EDUCATION, SOCIETY AND CULTURE

DR. SRUTIRUPA PANDA

ISBN 979-888569452-0

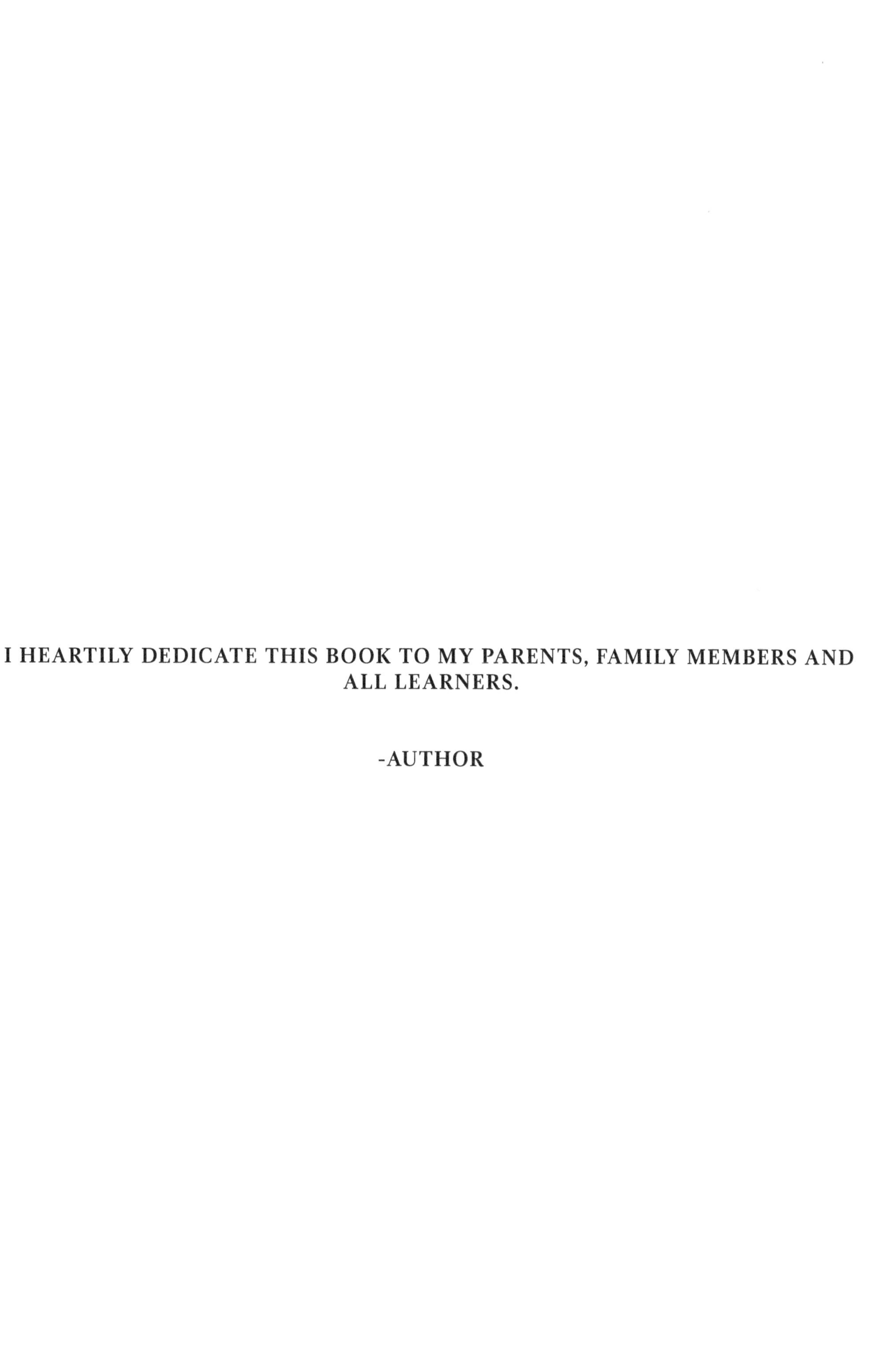

I HEARTILY DEDICATE THIS BOOK TO MY PARENTS, FAMILY MEMBERS AND ALL LEARNERS.

-AUTHOR

Contents

Preface   *vii*

  1. Society As A System   1

  2. Education As An Instrument Of Social Change   8

  3. Education And Modernization   17

  4. Education And Culture   25

  5. Diversity In Society   31

  6. Inequality   42

  7. Discrimination And Marginalization   49

  8. Role Of Education, School And Teacher   57

  9. Constitutional Provisons, Policies And Acts In Education   71

  10. Child Rights And Human Rights   77

References   87

Preface

Education, Society and Culture are strongly interrelated to each other. Teachers play pivotal role in preparing equal, impartial and democratic society for tomorrow. Hence they need to understand society as a system and education, culture, school as subsystem of society before practicing teaching professon. This book provides indepth idea to teachers regarding various concepts related to society, culture, social diversity, marginalization, discrimination, inequality and role of education, school, teachers to address various social issues. This book is prepared referring two year B.Ed. syllabus of SCERT. Odisha. It is expected that this book can be served as a guiding light for pre service and In service teachers to learn concepts related to above social issues

CHAPTER ONE

Society as a System

Society is condidered as unit system consisisting of several sub systems including school, culture, education etc.The term 'system' implies an orderly arrangement, an interrelationship of parts. In the arrangement, every part has a fixed place and definite role to play. The parts are bound by interaction. To understand the functioning of a system, for example the human body, one has to analyse and identify the sub-systems (e.g. circulatory, nervous, digestive, excretionary systems etc.) and understand how these various subsystems enter into specific relations in the fulfillment of the organic function of the body.

Likewise, society may be viewed as a system of interrelated mutually dependent parts which cooperate to preserve a recognisable whole and to satisfy some purposes or goal. Social system may be described as an arrangement of social interactions based on shared norms and values. Individuals constitute it and each has place and function to perform within it.

Meaning of Social System:

A social system basically consists of two or more individuals interacting directly or indirectly in a bounded situation. There may be physical or territorial boundaries, but the fundamental sociological point of reference is that the individuals are oriented, in a whole sense, to a common focus or inter-related foci. Thus, it is appropriate to regard such diverse sets of relationships as small groups, political parties and whole societies as social systems.

Social systems are open systems, exchanging information with, frequently acting with reference to other systems. Modern conceptions of the term can be traced to the leading social analysts of the 19th century, notably Auguste Comte, Karl Marx, Herbert Spencer and Emile Durkheim each of whom elaborated in some form or other conceptions of the major units of social systems (mainly societies) and the relationships between such units even though the expression social system was not a key one.

It is Talcott Parsons who has given the concept of 'system' current in modern sociology. Social system refers to' an orderly arrangement, an inter relationships of parts. In the arrangement, every part has a fixed place and definite role to play. The parts are bound by interaction. System signifies, thus, patterned relationship among constituent parts of a structure which is based on functional relations and which makes these parts active and binds them into reality.Society is a system of usages, authority and mutuality based on "We" felling and likeness. Differences within the society are not excluded. These are, however, subordinated to likeness. Inter-dependence and cooperation are its basis. It is bound by reciprocal awareness. It is essentially a pattern for imparting the social behaviour.

It consists in mutual inter action and interrelation of individuals and of the structure formed by their relations. It is not time bound. It is different from an aggregate of people and community. According to Lapiere, "The term society refers not to group of people, but to the complex pattern of the norms of inter action that arises among and between them."

Applying these conclusions to society, social system may be described as an arrangement of social interactions based on shared norms and values. Individuals constitute it, and each has place and function to perform within it. In the process, one influences the other; groups are formed and they gain influence, numerous subgroup come into existence.

But all of these are coherent. They function as a whole. Neither individual, nor the group can function in isolation. They are bound in oneness, by norms and values, culture and shared behaviour. The pattern that thus comes into existence becomes the social system.

A social system may be defined, after Parsons, a plurality of social actors who are engaged in more or less stable interaction "according to shared cultural norms and meanings" Individuals constitute the basic interaction units. But the interacting units may be groups or organisation of individuals within the system.

The social system, according to Charles P. Loomis, is composed of the patterned interaction of visual actors whose' relation to each other are mutually oriented through the definition of the mediation of pattern of structured and shared symbols and expectations.

All social organisations are, therefore, 'social system', since they consist of interacting individuals. In the social system each of the interacting individual has function or role to perform in terms of the status he occupies in the system. For example, in the family parents, sons and daughters are required to perform certain socially recognised functions or roles.

Similarly, social organisations function within the frame work of a normative pattern. Thus, a social system presupposes a social structure consisting of different parts which are interrelated in such a way as to perform its functions.

Social system is a comprehensive arrangement. It takes its orbit all the diverse subsystems such as the economic, political, religious and others and their interrelation too. Social systems are bound by environment such as geography. And this differentiates one system from another.

Elements of Social System:

The elements of social system are described as under:

1. Faiths and Knowledge:

The faiths and knowledge brings about the uniformity in the behaviour. They act as controlling agency of different types of human societies. The faiths or the faith is the result of the prevalent customs and beliefs. They enjoy the force of the individual are guided towards a particular direction.

2. Sentiment:

Man does not live by reason alone. Sentiments – filial, social, notional etc. have played immense role in investing society with continuity. It is directly linked with the culture of the people.

3. End Goal or object:

Man is born social and dependent. He has to meet his requirements and fulfill his obligations. Man and society exist between needs and satisfactions, end and goal. These determine the nature of social system. They provided the pathway of progress, and the receding horizons.

4. Ideals and Norms:

The society lays down certain norms and ideals for keeping the social system intact and for determining the various functions of different units. These norms prescribe the rules and regulations on the basis of which individuals or persons may acquire their cultural goals and aims.

In other words ideals and norms are responsible for an ideal structure or system of the society. Due to them the human behaviour does not become deviant and they act according to the norms of the society. This leads to organization and stability. These norms and ideals include folkways, customs, traditions, fashions, morality, religion, etc.

5. Status-Role:

Every individual in society is functional. He goes by status-role relation. It may come to the individual by virtue of his birth, sex, caste, or age. One may achieve it on the basis of service rendered.

6. Role:

Like the status, society has prescribed different roles to different individuals. Sometimes we find that there is a role attached to every status. Role is the external expression of the status. While discharging certain jobs or doing certain things, every individual keeps in his mind his status. This thing leads to social integration, organization and unity in the social system. In fact statuses and roles go together. It is not possible to separate them completely from one another.

7. Power:

Conflict is a part of social system, and order is its aim. It is implicit, therefore, that some should be invested with the power to punish the guilty and reward those who set an example. The authority exercising power will differ from group to group; while the authority of father may be supreme in the family, in the state it is that of the ruler.

8. Sanction:

It implies confirmation by the superior in authority, of the acts done be the subordinate or the imposition of penalty for the infringement of the command. The acts done or not done according to norms may bring reward and punishment.

Characteristics of Social System:

Social system has certain characteristics. These characteristics are as follows:

1. System is connected with the plurality of Individual actors:

It means that a system or social system cannot be borne as a result of the activity of one individual. It is the result of the activities of various individuals. For system, or social system, interaction of several individuals has to be there.

2. Aim and Objective:

Human interactions or activities of the individual actors should not be aimless or without object. These activities have to be according to certain aims and objects. The expression of different social relations borne as a result of human interaction.

3. Order and Pattern amongst various Constituent Units:

Mere coming together of various constituent units that from social system does not necessarily create a social system. It has to be according to a pattern, arrangement and order. The underlined unity amongst various constituent units brings about 'social system'.

4. Functional Relationship is the Basis of Unity:

We have already seen different constituent units have a unity in order to form a system. This unity is based on functional relations. As a result of functional relationships between different constituent units an integrated whole is created and this is known as social system.

5. Physical or Environmental Aspect of Social System:

It means that every social system is connected with a definite geographical area or place, time, society etc. In other words it means that social system is not the same at different times, at different place and under different circumstances. This characteristic of the social system again point out towards its dynamic or changeable nature.

6. Linked with Cultural System:

Social system is also linked with cultural system. It means that cultural system bring about unity amongst different members of the society on the basis of cultures, traditions, religions etc.

7. Expressed and implied Aims and Objects:

Social system is also linked with expressed and implied aims. In other words, it means that social system is the coming together of different individual actors who are motivated by their aims and objectives and their needs.

8. Characteristics of Adjustment:

Social system has the characteristic of adjustment. It is a dynamic phenomenon which is influenced by the changes caused in the social form. We have also seen that the social system is influenced by the aims, objects and the needs of the society. It means that the social system shall be relevant only if it changes itself according to the changed objects and needs. It has been seen that change takes place in the social system due to human needs, environment and historical conditions and phenomena.

9. Order, Pattern and Balance:

Social system has the characteristics of pattern, order and balance. Social system is not an integrated whole but putting together of different units. This coming together does not take place in a random and haphazard manner. There is an order am' balance.

It is so because different units of the society do not work as independent units but they do not exist in a vacuum but in a socio-cultural pattern. In the pattern different units have different functions and roles. It means that there is a pattern and order in the social system.

Types of Social System:

Parsons presents a classification of four major types in terms of pattern variable. These are as follows:

1. The Particularistic Ascriptive Type:

According to Parsons, this type of social system tends to be organized around kinship and sociality. The normative patterns of such a system are traditional and thoroughly dominated by the elements of ascription. This type of system is mostly represented by preliterate societies in which needs are limited to biological survival.

2. The Particularistic Achievement Type:

There is a significant role of religious ideas as differentiating element in social life. When these religious ideas are rationally systematized that possibility of new religious concepts emerge. As a result of this nature of prophecy and secondly it may depend on non-empirical realm to which the porphyry is connected.

3. The Universalistic Achievement Type:

When ethical prophecy and non-empirical conceptions are combined, a new set of ethical norms arise. It is because the traditional order is challenged by the ethical prophet in the name of supernatural. Such norms are derived from the existing relations of social member; therefore they are universalistic in nature. Besides, they are related with empirical or non-empirical goals, therefore they are achievement oriented.

4. The Universalistic Ascription Type:

Under this social type, elements of value orientation are dominated by the elements of ascription. Therefore emphasis is placed on status of the actor, rather than his performance. In such a system, actor's achievements are almost values to a collective goal. Therefore such a system becomes politicized and aggressive. An authoritarian State example of this types.

Maintenance of Social System:

A social system is maintained by the various mechanisms of social control. These mechanisms maintain the equilibrium between the various processes of social interaction.

In brief, these mechanisms may be classified in the following categories:

1. Socialization.

2. Social control.

(1) Socialization:

It is process by which an individual is adjusted with the conventional pattern of social behaviour. A child by birth is neither social nor unsocial. But the process of socialization develops him into a functioning member of society. He adjusts himself with the social situations conforming with social norms, values and standards.

(2) Social Control:

Like socialisation, social control is also a system of measures by which society moulds its members to conform with the approved pattern of social behaviour. According to Parsons, there are two types of elements which exist in every system. These are integrative and disintegrative and create obstacles in the advancement of integration.

Functions of Social System:

Social system is a functional arrangement. It would not exist if it were not so. Its functional character ensures social stability and continuity. The functional character of society, Parsons has discussed in depth. Other sociologists such as Robert F. Bales too have discussed it.

It is generally agreed that the social system has four primary functional problems to attend. These are:

1. Adaptation,

2. Goal attainment,

3. Integration,

4. Latent Pattern-Maintenance.

1. Adaptation:

Adaptability of social system to the changing environment is essential. No doubt, a social system is the result of geographical environment and a long drawn historical process which by necessity gives it permanence and rigidity. Yet, that should not make it wooden and inelastic. It need be a flexible and functional phenomenon.

Economy for its maintenance, division of labour for better production of goods and effective services, and role differentiation for job opportunity is essential. Durkheim in Division of Labour in society has given great attention to the role of division of labour and role differentiation as these make possible a higher average degree of skill than would otherwise be possible.

Lack of adaptability, very often has caused the social system to be challenged. It has caused revolution resulting in the overhauling of the system. The British system, in the nineteenth century, when the continent was in the inferno of revolution, showed remarkable adaptability. It responded well to the mounting demands of change. Over the time our system has demonstrated the excellent sense of adaptability.

2. Goal Attainment:

Goal attainment and adaptability are deeply interconnected. Both contribute to the maintenance of social order.

Every social system has one or more goals to be attained through cooperative effort. Perhaps the best example of a societal goal is national security. Adaptation to the social and nonsocial environment is, of course, necessary if goals are to be attained. But in addition, human and nonhuman resources must be mobilised in some effective way, according to the specific nature of tasks.

For example, there must be a process of ensuring that enough persons, but not too many, occupy each of the roles at a particular time and a process for determining which persons will occupy which roles. These processes together solve the problem of allocation of members in the social system. We have already touched upon the "need" for property norms. The rules regulating inhcritance e.g., primogeniture-in part solve this problem.

The allocation of members and the allocation of scarce valuable resources are important, of course, for both adaptation and goal attainment. The difference between adaptation and goal attainment is a relative one.

The economy of a society is that subsystem which produces goods and services for a wide variety of purposes; the "polity", which includes above all the Government in complex societies, mobilizes goods and services for the attainment of specific goals of the total society regarded as a single social system.

3. Integration:

Social system is essentially an integration system. In the general routine of life, it is not the society but the group or the subgroup in which one feels more involved and interested. Society, on the whole does not come into one's calculations. Yet, we know as indicated by Durkheim, that individual is the product of society. Emotions, sentiments and historical forces are so strong that one cannot cut oneself from his moorings.

The working of these forces is best seen when society is involved in a domestic crisis or an external challenge. An appeal in the name of society, culture, heritage, patriotism, national solidarity or social welfare invokes quick response. Cooperation in effort is often demonstrative of integrating. It is the real basis of integration.

During normal times, the spirit of integration is best expressed by not disregarding the regulative norms. Abiding by them is essential, as otherwise, it will be the domination of might over right, of self over society, and the spirit of mutuality which is based on common welfare, will get eliminated. The command and obedience relation as it exists is based on rationality and order. If it is not sustained, the social order would break down.

In almost every social system, and in every system as large as a society, some participants, including whole subgroups, violate the relational or regulative norms. So far as these norms meet social needs, violations are a threat to the social system,

This necessitates the need for social control. "Social control" is the need for standardized reactions to violations in order to protect the integrity of the system. When there is dispute concerning the interpretation of relational or regulative norms, or concerning the factual aspects of conflicts of interest, there is need for agreed-upon social arrangements for settling the dispute. Otherwise the social system would be subject to progressive splits.

4. Latent Pattern-maintenance:

Pattern maintenance and tension management is the primary function of social system. In absence of appropriate effort in this direction maintenance and continuity of social order is not possible. In fact within every social system there is the in built mechanism for the purpose.

Every individual and subgroup learns the patterns in the process of the internalization of norms and values. It is to invest the actors with appropriate attitude and respect towards norms and institution, that the socialization works. It is not; however, merely the question of imparting the pattern, equally essential is to make the actor to follow it. For this there is always a continuous effort -in operational terms of social control.

There may yet be occasions when the components of social system may become subject of distraction and disturbance. Tension may arise due to internal or external causes and society may get involved into a critical situation. Just as a family in distress draws upon all its resources to overcome it, so also society has to overcome it.

This process of 'overcoming' is the management of the tension. Society has the responsibility, like a family, to keep its members functional, to relieve them of anxiety, to encourage those who would be detrimental to the entire system. The decline of societies has been very much because the pattern maintenance and tension management mechanism has often failed.

Equilibrium and Social Change:

Equilibrium is a state of 'balance'. It is "a state of just poise". The term is used to describe the interaction of units in a system. A state of equilibrium exists, when systems tend towards conditions of minimum stress and least imbalance. The existence of balance between units facilitates the normal operation of system. Community evaluates and recognises the importance of equilibrium.

The equilibrium condition, is a "condition of integration and stability". It is sometimes made possible with the development of a certain set of productive forces such as pressure groups which brings into being an appropriate super structure of institutions. Equilibrium can also be of moving sort, which according to Parsons, is "an orderly process of change of the system".

The maintenances of equilibrium, according to him resolve two fundamental types of process: "The first of these are the process of the socialization by which actors acquire the orientations necessary to the performance of their roles in the social systems, when they have not previously possessed them; the second type are the process involved in the balance between the generation of motivations to deviate behaviour and the counter balancing motivations to restoration of the stabilized interactive process which we have called mechanism of social control".

A social system implies order among the interacting units of the systems. This order, be it equilibrium or harmonious relations between individuals, is likely to be disturbed, at times, by social changes, occasioned by innovations which force new conceptions of roles and norms. The role of a housewife is affected when she goes for work away from home. This change is bound to influence other social institutions as well.

Maintaining the orderliness or social system is difficult when social changes are frequent. Herbert Spencer introduced the cause and effect relationships to explain the changing nature of societies in the equilibrium/ disequilibrium' analysis.

The structural-functional pattern of institutions which constitute a society would change in accordance with change it may encounter in its total external environment, and with changes in its internal conditions. There would be a changing disposition of the parts of a society until some appropriate 'equilibrium' is reached.

Spencer elaborating the theory of equilibrium has indicated its universal applicability. He pointed out that members of a society are continuously in the process of adapting to its material substance. "Each society", he wrote, "displays the process of equilibration in the continuous adjustment of its population to its means of subsistence.

A tribe of men living on wild animals and fruits is manifestly like every tribe of inferior creatures, always oscillating from side to side of that average number which the locality can support. Thought by artificial production unceasingly improved, a superior race continually alters the limit which external conditions put to population, yet there is ever a checking of population at the temporary limit reached".

In elaborating his theory of equilibrium, Spencer has referred to several economic aspects, and to the industrial system, of a society which continuously adjusts itself to the forces of 'supply and demand'. He has also discussed political institutions in 'equilibrium-disequilibrium' terms. It is applicable to, all societies equally.

Taking society as a total entity, and its interrelationship with its parts, the changes in them can be explained by 'equilibrium- disequilibrium' adjustments. "Marxian Historical Materialism" remarks Ronald Fletcher, in The

Making of Sociology is in fact an" equilibrium-disequilibrium analysis of the historical sequences of social order and social changes, and the explanation of this process in terms of material changes, attendant social conflict, and its resolution."

Education as a Sub-system of Society:

Education is a sub-system in the wider social system. Some of these systems include education boards, institutes, colleges and schools. Education is responsible for the transfer of skills and knowledge from one person to the other.

It has linkages with the economic, political, religious, and other sub-systems which exert powerful influence on the goals and instrumentalities of the educational sub-system on the one hand and on its autonomy on the other. Education can rarely free itself from social and cultural norms and has to relate itself to the ferments within the society.

The educational sub-system is not the only agency offering education, to begin with, the domestic group, the neighborhood, and the peer group has important educational roles and the educational process continues beyond the formal school stage through books, mass media, cultural, political, and religious intercourse and interpersonal contacts of a wide variety. The formal education system has to take account of early socialization and has to anticipate future educational processes.

The characteristics of education as a social sub-system:

- It helps to turn society in the right direction.
- Education system emerges as a final outcome of the working and dynamics of different institutions of society.
- Educations become the essential agent in building social individualism.
- Educational institutions provide one to interact with the people from the other castes and culture.

CHAPTER TWO

Education as an Instrument of Social Change

Social Change

Acc to Prof. RB Mathur (1964)

"Social Change refers to the modifications in the organization and behavior of the grop expressed in its laws, institutions, customs, modes and beliefs. When change supposedly for the better it becomes progress which is essentially an evolutionary concept"

According to SP Ruhela

" The term social change might imply changes in social attitudes, behavior, customs, habits, manners, relations and value of people, in social institutions and structures, in the ways or styles of living"

"Education is the most powerful weapon which you can use to change the world." said Nelson Mandela. Education is the median through which we can change the world. It helps us to turn weakness into strength, failure into success. It helps us in identifying problems present around us in our society and also helps us in searching for their solutions.

It helps us in increasing the mental ability of a person which in turn changes the way a person thinks. This results in the change of pattern of social relationship and hence, it may cause social change. One of the main impetus of education is to change the attitude, thinking and lifestyle of a person.

According to Britannica, social change refers to the alteration of mechanisms within the social structure, characterized by changes in cultural symbols, rules of behaviour, social organizations, or value systems.

Hence, it means that to change man is to change a society only. When a person gets educated, he/she knows that what is right or wrong. Thus, education not only prepares a person for social change but also encourages an individual to proceed in the direction of social change.

Our Indian history had a number of important and notable social reformers like Swami Vivekanand, Raja Ram Mohan Roy, Rabindranath Tagore and Mahatma Gandhi who took an important role in the process of bringing out social changes. Many reform movements were led by these reformers.

According to Collins Dictionary, reform consists of changes and improvements to a law, social system, or institution. All the reformers felt the need of a strong and sound education system for social change. Education brings change in every aspect of a person's life and hence, education can be regarded as the perfect instrument for social change.

Types of Social change

Progressive/ Positive

The change from social evils to scientific thoughts

Digressive / Negative

In a well going society new evils emerg

NATURE OF SOCIAL CHANGE

1. A Universal Phenomenon

2. The spreading of social change is not uniform

3. Variations in the Speed of social change

4. Unpredictable

5. Results in interaction of number of factors

6. Modifications or replacements.

Aspects of Social Change

Social

Economic

Political

Religious

Scientific and Technological

Factors affecting Social Change

Factors Leading to Social Changes

The stimulating factors which are responsible for bringing about social changes in a society are the following

Demographic Factors: Changes in the size and composition of the population are undoubtedly a very important factor leading to social change. The rapid growth of population brings about many changes in the standard of living as well as changes in the social structures and organization of the society.

Biological Factors: Due to the problem of conflict between generations there is always a scope for new patterns to emerge. No new generation ever exactly reenact the social life of its predecessor leading to rejection of some aspects of social life while acceptation and innovation of some others.

Technological Factors: Technological developments play an important role in societal changes as they transform the structure of the whole society. These rapid technological advancements bring about many changes in the attitudes, beliefs and even in traditions of the society.

Natural Factors: Man can never have complete control over nature as none can claim to regulate the weather which greatly affects our mode of thinking, traditions, customs, eating habits, clothing, etc. Moreover it is difficult to achieve technologicaldevelopments in a country lacking in the natural resources.

Legislations: Law is dynamic. It brings about social change by influencing behavior, beliefs and values.

Psychological Factors: Human nature always wants a change. He does not want to be tied to the same environment, same customs, traditions and same cultural values. Human beings welcome innovation for the development and betterment of the society. As a result of these changes modernization takes place

1) Cultural factors

2) Geographical factors

3) Environmental factors

4) Economic factors

5) Factor of migration

6) Technological factor

7) Factor of population

8) Psychological factor

9) Ideological factors

10) Factor of war

11) Diffusion of cultures

12) Urbanization

13) Visual and print media

14) Westernization

15) Industrialization

16) Actions of exceptional individuals

17) Legislation

18) Secularism

19) Democratization

20) Materialistic attitude

Obstacles in Social Change

1. Superstitious beliefs
2. Conservative nature
3. Cultural fanaticism
4. Castes
5. Classism
6. Religion
7. Fear
8. Regionalism
9. Parochialism
10. Isolation

Role of education in society

Education has a great social importance especially in the modern, complex industrialized societies. The main social objective of education is to complete the socialization process. The school and other institutions have come into being in place of family to complete the socialization process.

Education acts asintegrative force in society by communicating value that unite different sections of society. The family may fail to provide the child the essential knowledge of the social skills and values of the wider society. Education helps the child to develop the inborn potentialities of child providing scope to develop. Education helps to modify the past behavior through learning and through different agencies of education. Education aims at the all-round development of childphysical, mental, social, emotional, and spiritual. After completion of education the child can earn its livelihood getting proper education, which has productivity. The education should be imparted according to the own interest of the child. The whole personality of the child is developed physically, intellectually, morally, socially, aesthetically and spiritually. He is recognized in the society

Education as an Instrument of Social Change

Education has a great social importance especially in the modern, complex industrialized societies. It is one of the concrete sources from which one gets information and knowledge. It affects the society. The role of education as an instrument or agent of social change and social development is widely accepted in the present society. Society needs to change from time to time for its own prosperity and development. Social change may include changes in nature, social institutions, social behaviours, or social relations. Change means accepting new ideas leading to evolution and development. Social change takes place as a result of many types of changes that takes place in the social and nonsocial environment.

Change is inevitable in a society. Education in every sense is one of the fundamental factors of development. No country can achieve sustainable economic development without substantial investment in human capital. Education enriches people's understanding of themselves and world. It improves the quality of their lives and leads to broad social benefits to individuals and society. Education is an instrument on social change and development which constitutes an essential input into the development process itself. The role of education in the development of human resources in particular, requires hardly and emphasis. Education raises people's productivity and creativity and promotes entrepreneurship and technological advances. Additionally, it plays a very crucial role in securing economic and social progress and improving income distribution. Education plays a major role in eradicating poverty by granting access to different employment opportunities. Education system needs to be upgraded time to time to incorporate desired changes in order to cope with the present changes in the society. Education system should be made more practical rather than providing mere theoretical knowledge. Rather than learning only the theoretical aspects practical knowledge should be provided. The use of information and communication technology (ICT) brings about a powerful learning environment and it transforms the learning and teaching process in which students deal with knowledge in an active, self-directed and constructive way (Volman and Eck, 2001). ICT is not only considered as a tool, which can be added for existing teaching methods but also nowadays ICT is seen as an important instrument to support new ways of teaching learning process. In this 21st century, the term "technology" is an important issue in many fields including education. This isbecause technology has become the knowledge transfer highway in most countries.

The role of education as an instrument of social change is widely recognized today.

- Education can initiate change by bringing about a change in the outlook and attitudes of a person.
- It can bring about a change in the pattern of social relationship and thereby, it may cause social changes. One of the purposes of education is to change person and his life and living style. To change man is to change society only.
- Social changes may begin at unconscious level but soon may be promoted to the conscious level. The changes, however, do not remain at unconscious level for a long time.
- They may be initiated at unconscious level but their acceptance takes place at conscious level and it is only at this level that the changes become universally acceptable in a group, a society or a nation. Education has a dual role to perform.
- First, it creates frustration in the individual with the existing situation. It prepares him to look for change, It promotes dejection, thus, unconsciously, it prepares the people towards accepting change whenever it is to be presented.
- Secondly, education simply does not stop at the preparation of the individual for a change. It also enables the individual to proceed in the direction of bringing about changes in the society at conscious level.
- There are number of social reformers namely, Raja Ram Mohan Roy, Swami Vivekananda, Mahatma Gandhi who made all the efforts at the basic level to bring out the social changes.
- All the reformers felt the need of sound education system to match with the rapid scenario of the social change in the society.
- A reform movement is distinguished from more radical social movements such as revolutionary movements. A reform movement is a kind of social movement that aims to make gradual change, or change in certain aspects of society rather than rapid or fundamental changes.
- British education became solidified into India as missionary schools were established during the 1920s. New policies in 1835 gave rise to the use of English as a medium of education.Under the British rule in India, education was imparted through the medium of English. It not only deprived the people of the knowledge of their own language and literature.But also wasted the precious time of the youth in cramming the rules of grammar of a foreign language. The pattern of education developed in India during the British rule was unplanned.
- Earlier educational institutions and teachers used to show a specific way of life to the students and education was more a means of social control than an instrument of social change. Modern educational institutions do not place much emphasis upon transmitting a way of life to the students.
- The traditional education was meant for an unchanging static society not marked by any change. But today, education aims at imparting knowledge. Education was associated with religion.
- It has become secular today. It is an independent institution now. Education has been chiefly instrumental in preparing the way for the development of science and technology.
- Education has brought about phenomenal changes in every aspect of person's life. Francis J. Brown remarks that education is a process which brings about changes in the behavior of society.
- It is a process which enables every individual to effectively participate in the activities of society and to make positive contribution to the progress of society.

According to the Education Commission (1964-66), the view of the important role of education in the national development and in building up a truly democratic society.

The Government considered it necessary to survey and examine the entire field of education in order to realize a well balanced, integrated and adequate system of national education capable of making a powerful contribution to all aspects of national life.

Role of education in Social Change

1) Education perpetuates eternal values
2) Promotes capacity to welcome social change
3) Evaluation of social change
4) Transmission of culture
5) Removal of obstacles
6) Increasing the areas of knowledge
7) Leadership role
8) Mother of new changes
9) Spreading knowledge
10) Stabilizing democratic values
11) Control channelizes and modifies thoughts of new generation
12) School as a workshop for citizenship training
13) Awareness against social evils
14) National and international understanding
15) Equality among masses
16) Social Awakening
17) National Development

Education and Cultural Change

All cultures are inherently predisposed to change and, at the same time, to resist change. There are dynamic processes operating in a society that encourages the acceptance of new ideas and changes. When changes take place for progress they are readily accepted by the society for its well-being. Within a society cultural changes take place as a result of diffusion which is the movement of things and ideas from one culture to another. Culture loss is an inevitable result of old cultural patterns being replaced by new ones. In this process major changes take place which lead to progressive changes for the welfare of the society. Education can cut down the thick roots of traditions, superstitions, ignorance and backwardness etc. When diffusion takes place the form of a trait may move from one society to another but not its original cultural meaning. Within a society, processes leading to change include invention and culture loss. Inventions may be either 4 technological or ideological which include inventions of new tools, scientific instruments or transportation methods etc. or invention of new mathematical theorems. Education can prepare the society for the cultural imbalances that inevitably characterize the social transitional situation, and should endeavour to prevent, as far as possible, shocking conditions, and, during the long transitional phase, it can discipline the people to withhold immediate gratification in the interest of future inputs for the furtherance of the long-range plans of modernization. Education and social change Social change means change in social structure: the nature, the social institutions, the social behaviour or the social relations of a society, community of people, and so on.

Education and social change are interrelated. Both are equally important for the growth and development of a society. Education and social change is a two-way process. While education is responsible for preservation, transmission and dissemination of the whole culture, social change is the instrument and precondition of educational thought. Education initiatesthe social change and gives them direction and purpose. Education prepares the individual for social changes. Education determines the nature of social changes, which ought to be brought about. Education is the most powerful instrument to bring about social revolution. Education for all, at all levels, and at all ages of children is the only remedy to bring about the desired social change in any society. The relationship between education and social change takes a dual form-education as an instrument and education as a product. Education as an instrument is used as a means for bringing about desired changes in the society and in the latter case changes in the educational structure follows as a consequence of changes which have already taken place in the society.

There are three types of relationship between education and social change which are as follows:

1. Education as a Necessary Condition of Social Change Historical experience of advanced countries has shown that for any social revolution education is the pre-condition. Illiterates remain satisfied with their existing conditions

and feel that they are destined to be what they are. They never bother to exert to bring change in their present social and economic conditions. They are guided by orthodoxy, traditions and fate rather than by rationality in their actions. Education helps people to make them rational in their thinking and approach.

2. Education as an Outcome of Social Change There is inter-dependent relationship between education and social change. On the one hand it brings change in social conditions. On the other hand it is influenced by social change, which means social change helps spreading education. Education follows social change. It has its place before and after social change First come social changes and then teaching process is changed according to those social changes. Education system changes according to the needs of society.

3. Education as an Instrument of Social Change Education as an instrument of social change means how education helps people to bring social change. Education changes the outlook and the tradition approach towards social and economic problems. It sharpens the skills andknowledge of the children. Technical education helps in the process of industrialization which results in vast changes in society. Education not only preserves the cultural traditions i.e., customs, traditions and values etc. of the society but also transmits them to the next generation. It also motivates the children to adopt new pattern in order to remain dynamic and forward looking. Education fulfils the needs of the society and propagates such ideas which promote social changes in all fields of life.Society has undergone vast transformation through several ages. New ideas have emerged and social changes have been brought about by both individual and collective actions. Changes in a society are inevitable due to the existence and amalgamation of different cultures, languages and religions in a society. As a result of these social change cultural changes takes place. Social change is an alteration which occurs in the structure and function.

Influence of Education on Family

According to Maciver

" *A family is a group defined by a sex relationship sufficiently precise an enduring to provide for procreation and bringing of children*"

A family unit is the unit which builds up a person's personality. How you behave and what you become in life is very much dependent on your family life. Psychologists believe that a child learns the most from his or her family life

According to Burgess and locke

" *A family is a group of person united by the ties of marriage, blood or adoption constituting a single household, interacting and intercommunicating with each other*"

. The way your family members deal with you has a lifelong effect on your personality. Keeping in view all these facts the importance of your family life cannot be denied. Family unit happens to be the most important part of your life till you grow up. The children are usually closer to their parents and their siblings as compared to any other person in the world. As the children grow up they find good friends, spouses, their own kids and colleagues to share their lives with. Although time brings this change but the importance of family remains there. The children who have a sound family background and who belong to a family with strong family ties are almost always happier. Thus one cannot deny the importance of family life.

Types of Family

Extended Family: The unit in which the adults and children of more than two generations are closely combined. The family in this system extend vertically over three or more generations.

Nuclear Family: The nuclear family is a small unit consisting of parents and children usually two. In this unit the parents are sole authorities and emotional relations among family members are concentrated and intense

Roles Of family

1. Cooperation of family in education
2. Proper Physical Development
3. Proper moral development
4. Blossoming the interest of children
5. Opportunity to participate in household responsibilities
6. Development of intellect

7. Free expression of child's desires and urges

8. Religious education

Influence of Education on Family

1. Improve home management

2. Recognition of worth of home

3. Production of educated elite (Families)

4. To discharge productive duties towards home

5. Family Planning

6. An efficient member of family

7. Social efficiency of family

8. Adjustability in family

9. Co-ordination of family and school

10. Education of parents

11. To maintain better homes

12. Cultivation of higher values

13. Propagates cooperation within and outside the home

14. Create liberal and wider attitude

15. Increasing productivity of family members

16. Optimizing Economic efficiency

Influence of Education on society

Education plays a very important role in moulding the character of an individual. It is one of the concrete sources from which one get information and knowledge. It affects the society. We can make sense of its effective role from the following points.

1] *Preservation and transmission of our social, moral and cultural values.*

In Education, through curriculum, students will be acquainted with social, moral and cultural values and teachers make them familiar with values and ideal through different activities, games, story-telling etc. Education makes them familiar with constitution, rules and regulations of citizens and so on. As we find in NPE 1986 major objectives to produce a productive citizen has been fulfilled by education so education preserves our value and it make others to imbibe those values.

2] *Awakening of Social feelings*

Through education individuals become aware about the importance of unity, love, fraternity and other values. Education makes all people get awakened of being a part of society and how they can contribute the world as society. People know different values and life skills and thus they develop concern for society including social mindedness, values life skills, learning to be, learning to do, learning to know, learning to live together via different activities story telling dramatization.

3] *Political development of society*

Education makes all aware about rights and duties of all, which are their responsibilities and duties so that they can develop their civic sense. Through different lesson of political leaders and stories education develop ideal leadership quality so that in future citizens can lead t e state as a society.

4] *Economic development of society*

Education develops skills in individual and makes him a productive citizen. Through education everyone learns how to earn money and as per their qualification he gets job or labour and on the whole with the help of education more or less everyone get work and earn money so due to increasing literacy per capita income will increase As we find govt take help in the form of tax and thus our economy develops. Because of education people migrate in other country and their earning helps to develop society, country. Thus education affects the economic development of society.

5] *Social control*

Education makes all aware about customs and duties the same as it makes aware about the rules and regulations as we find the rules in Indian constitution. People know how to preserve their lives via education. They make also familiar with crimes. Thus education provides a guideline and it controls all society.

6] *Social changes and reforms*

Education makes individuals perfects and aware about the rights. So can claim against dwelled superstitions, beliefs which are harmful for them. Through education everyone learn grow to live and how to save from difficulty and how to inculcate values and ideals in their lives and ideals in their lives so they can appeal in court having of felling injustice. Education makes all aware about how to live peacefully and how to face difficulties ion their lives .They become aware about the proverbs like 'nothing ventured, nothing gained' so they develop their risk taking attitudes via education.

7] *Socialization of a child*

Education trains the mind of a child and it teaches him how to inculcate values in his life. It makes the child understand what is society, how he is a part of society, what are his roles in society, how he should behave, how he should interact with others etc. Education helps him to understand who is he? And it develops a sense if a social being in him. In short education socializes a child.

Thus, education produces productive citizens it helps everyone how to flourish and makes them ideal citizens of society. To sum up, Education influences the society.

Functions of Education as an Instrument of Social Change

Education fulfils the needs of society and propagates such ideas which promote social change in all fields of life. In this way, education becomes a social process by means of which society moulds children according to its needs and approved patterns of behaviour. Functions of education as an instrument of social change are as follows:

(1) Stabilizing Eternal Values : Education protects eternal values, saves them from pernicious effects of social changes and promotes their knowledge and acceptance in such a manner that inspite of social changes, people in general keep faith in these values. In our society such eternal values are of moral and spiritual nature. Education should protect, preserve and promote these values.

(2) Increasing the Areas of Knowledge Education promotes in the individuals the capacity to increase the scope of knowledge more and more for their benefit. It opens new areas for investigations and researches, which bring about desirable changes in material as well as non-material aspects of culture. Thus education prepares ground for the advent of social change.

(3) Leadership Role in Social Change Education provides leadership in social change. Education makes people capable to initiate and guide for needed social changes by fighting successfully against social evils, customs and blind traditions. Thus, people become capable for realizingtheir own true personality to the full and promote social welfare to greater and greater extent.

(4) Evaluation of Social Change Education lays down the required standards and criteria of values with reference to which this process of evaluation takes place effectively, and only after that, desirable social changes are propagated where the undesirable ones discarded.

(5) Education Accelerates Social Change Education tries to banish social evils, blind customs and traditions through various social reformation projects, political movements, social service schemes and also tries to bring in 'needed social changes and reforms.

(6) Education Prepares People Mentally for Social Change It prepares the mentality of people to welcome and adopt desirable social changes easily. It may be noted that people will welcome and adopt any technique or

pattern only when they become convinced of its utility and desirability. Education, thus structures a wholesome and conducive environment for these social changes to become acceptable to all. It tries to remove the mental 8 reservations and complexes in the minds of people which obstruct the progress of change. Education provides necessary training in skills and occupations and thus produces the needed competent personnel for manning the different specialized jobs in modern industry, business, educational and research establishments and other secondary associations. Education is expected to change the values and attitudes of the people for the betterment of the society

Education in the Present Time and Social Change in India

There is no denying the fact that India, in the last six or seven decades , has given to the world a great number of number of scientists, academicians, intellectuals, innovators, professionals and technocrats who have not just excelled in their fields but also made a mark at the international levels. The present era is, however an era of great change and rapid technology that is changing every facet of life—and has posed some challenges as well as puzzles before Education. Today, it is a world of high competition and career focused individuals-both men and women-like never before. Now education has closely come to be synonymous with employability. And modern technology is the indispensible tool that is used heavily to give, provide and receive education. However,besides being employment-oriented, education should also aim at making modern technology accessible, acceptable and usable. India has a huge pool of population .Instead of viewing the growing population as a liability; it should be changed into an asset and an instrument to boost economic and social and growth. This can be done only through human development, which in turn is possible only by education . And this is where the challenges before the present educational system begins. The present education system needs some changes to fulfil the above goals. Some deficiencies in the present education system may be described as follows:

(1) The present education generates andfortifies, but only partially, the type of knowledge that is relevant and pertinent to our changing society.

(2) Technology associated with a particular stream of knowledge maybe inappropriate to the present stage of development in India, in terms of its employment potential or investment, or its widespread utility.

(3)The present information, speed, and vocation -centred education has completely failed to provide value framework which is vital to preparing honest, sincere, and conscientious citizens—who eventually take the country to the path of peace and progress. Education is a means as well as end by itself. It is not and it should not be a guarantee to achieve high status and higher positions to all people—nor can that be possible. But certainly it could be a facilitator to a quality life –to the means to provide all the basic amenities of a comfortable living, so that once, these are fulfilled, man can think of and work towards attaining self actualization, which is the ultimate aim of education .Moreover, in the rudimentary form, education also helps achieve social mobility. It also plays a significant role in equalizing opportunities in many ways, some of which are—

(1) By making it possible for all those who have the desire to be informed as well as enlightened citizens of their country, to receive and be benefitted by education.

(2) By promoting a scientific and objective outlook.

(3) By creating a social environment of acceptance of and mutual tolerance towards various religions, languages, castes, class, etc.

(4) by providing equal opportunities of social mobility to all individuals in society

CHAPTER THREE

Education and Modernization

What isModernization?

Modernization is a process of change from traditional and quasi-traditional order to certain desired types of technology. This can take place in values, social structure and achievements of the individual. This process is a holistic one, it affects the thinking process, the beliefs, value of the people as a whole.

"Modernization means the development of a modern outlook in everyday life." It does not mean the abandonment of religion and more acceptances of modern equipment's, tools and gadgets. Technological achievements and scientific advancement in developing countries is limited. The development of rational outlook and scientific approach is also limited. Still many aspects of socio- cultural life are still dominated by faith-oriented ideologies and traditions. It cannot be denied that the traditional approach is becoming significant and the traditional practices are being replaced by the modern ones. According to Deutch, "Modernization is a process in which major clusters of old social, economic and psychological commitments are eroded and broken and people become available for new pattern of socialization and behavior,"

Definitions of Modernizations

Jha(1978) described modernization as, "Modernization is total reorientation of man's belief, outlook and attitudes."

David (2003) Converses , " Modernization implies two things one transformation in material setting involving systems (political, economic and educational) and institutions, secondly it may also imply change to value system or value consensus.

The salient features of the modernization are:- It is a process of structural transformation of social, economic and political structures. It signifies a conscious process, a process of purposive and planned change. It implies transformation in the direction of increasing economic rationality, technological rapidity and structural elasticity. It is not a process of imitation but a process of identification with the advanced countries in the matter of material affluence and physical abundance. Material prosperity is to be attained by the progressive programs for the utilization of science and technologyIt involves either adoption or adaption of the modern scientific and technological characteristics in to the emerging patterns of modern nations. Standards of performance and achievements are to be accomplished by slow but sure degrees.

Advantages and Disadvantages of Modernization

The advantages and disadvantages of Modernization are as follows:

1. Culture: On the one hand, modernization has encouraged the development of new forms of creative expression, such as film and television .These forms can be easily exported and viewed all over the world .However, a loss of culture may result from modernization .The spread of the Western Culture has caused young people in non-Western countries to abandon their traditional customs and values .Even languages has begin to disappear as urbanization encourages people to learn a country's dominant language.

2. Business :New technology has revolutionized the speed and accuracy of production .furthermore ,increased global trade allows businesses to sell their products anywhere .But increased global production may hurt domestic business when international companies can offer products at cheaper prices .The production of goods in foreign countries ,where labor laws are more relaxed ,amounts to exploitation in some people's view.

3. Environment: National resources such as wood, water and oil are often processed in modernized society, and skyscrapers and factories begin to transform the landscape. Environmental problems, such as climate change, are believed to be the result of industrial development and production .However in many poorer countries, the discovery of oil and the adoption of new technologies is welcomed for the financial opportunities it presents. Communication and Travel: New inventions such as phones, televisions and computers allow people to communicate instantly anywhere on the globe .Increased global travel allows people to visit foreign cultures for business or leisure .Contact with foreign cultures fosters international cooperation, but can also result in further loss of culture as people begin to adopt the foreign cultures and languages they are exposed to. Education as an Instrument for Modernization The education commission of India under the chairmanship of Dr. D.S. Kothari (1966) had reiterated in clear and unambiguous terms that education is the main instrument of change in all fields of life of nation-social, cultural, economic, technological and industrial. It has realized the importance of education as instrument for national development. For education to perform its new task of modernizing the Indian society, the commission has suggested the following educational strategies: This can be done if education, if education, If education is related to productivity, If education strengthens social and national integration, If education consolidates democracy as a form of government and helps the country to adopt it as a way of life, hastens the process of modernization, and strives to build character by cultivating social, moral and spiritual values."

Modernization and Education

Education and modernization are closely linked. It is education that canserve as an efficient instrument for effective modernization for a nation to modernize itself, the spread of education in rapid strides is quite essential. The cream of intelligential is but the product education churning. Education is butanothername for human resource development. It produces the skilled personnel to occupy different positions in life who would contribute for the growth of national wealth through their creative abilities and productive efforts. The pace of education as such serves as an indication for the level of modernization a nation has attained. Education is the key that opens the doors of modernization in various fields of nation's life like economic, industrial, technological and social fields. How Modernization affects Education On the other side, Modernization process has its own implications for education. The impact of modernization on the educative process should be properly understood. Modernization demands that the teaching and testing technology should be modernized in order to achieve better quickly as possible. The development of science and technology has influenced teaching and testing procedures so much that they are considered as belonging to technology by themselves. Today the instructional technology makes use ofadvanced auto-visual aids, tape-recorders, movies a broadcasting net-work, television and, "teacher - in – the sky satellites." Especially worthy of mentioning are teaching machines and computer in the classroom. Unless and until we modernize the instruction techniques as done in the far advanced countries, our efforts for educating and modernizing the nation will not be far – fetching.

Certain visible parameters contribute directly to the process and pace of modernisation.

They are a sound political ideology and its effective operation, viable national economy, functionally literate population, wholesome personality, skilled man-power, modified values and motivation, concerted national efforts, open mindedness etc.

These are rightly regarded as the gifts of education. Education disseminates political ideology of a nation, expedites the growth of economy, prepares abled and skilled man-power and makes people literate functionally and expands the minds for the larger interests of the society and nation.

2. Education directly contributes to the process of modernisation. It is rightly acknowledged that human resource is the key to national advancement and a sound human resource is created and developed by education.

It produces the skilled persons with a sound knowledge base to occupy and operate economic, industrial, technological and social fields. This high -powered human resource contributes to the growth of national wealth through their creative abilities and productive efforts. Therefore, education promotes in the rising generation those knowledge, skills and attitudes which accelerate the pace of modernisation.

3. As a dynamic force of change education breaks the status quo of the traditional thinking, doing, habits, attitudes and values. It broadens the mental horizon are arouses interest in innovation and experimentation. It helps

Individuals to be broad-minded and stimulates their thinking to accept new things and objects without a compromise with the old thinking and ideas.

4. Education creates a cadre of philosophers, scientists, technocrats, leaders, elite, co-planners, administrators, physician, teachers etc. who vanguard the chariot of modernisation. They are highly sensitive to the needs, demands and aspirations of, a modernized society and they work for consensus building on important issues including national and emotional integration, and above all international understanding.

They socialize individuals to look at the objects, ideas, things, persons etc. in the correct perspectives by cultivating scientific temper and fostering rationality. These two cardinal instruments i.e. scientific temper and spirit and rational thinking help man to evaluate everything in its correct forms and perspectives.

Therefore, a society is advanced in every respects and education is the originator and creator of every things which steers the vehicle of modernisation.

5. Education, as a chief instrument of modernisation arouses, sustains, stimulates and perpetuates interest in the minds of people in the change and growth processes. Education helps in the evolution of mind which is dispassionate, and objective and enquiring.

Education brings about change in the mind: attitude, value, opinion etc. to work for the progress and prosperity of a nation. Moreover, education helps in the increase of production and income of a nation. Therefore, there is a positive correlation between education and the growth of per capita and national income. Education is rightly called as the engine of economic growth of a nation.

6. Education prepares a band of knowledgeable and creative men and women by imparting appropriate value, skill and knowledge adequately who, in turn, will commit themselves to the process of modernisation. Thus, modernisation is harnessed by education.

7. Education acts as a powerful force of modernisation by developing national outlook and international understanding. It can help the pupils in knowing the latest developments in social, economic, technological, scientific and cultural domains of human life.

8. Education can help in the achievement of emotional and national integration which is the basis for establishing unity among people and for development of nation-social, cultural, economic and political and scientific aspects.

9. Education can help in accelerating the process of modernisation by fostering a democratic and secular outlook and vision among the people. Secular attitude helps in developing respect for all religions of the world and of the nation. Democratic altitude enables people to live successfully in the society with others without any difference and feelings.

10. Education helps people to prepare for future life winch is essential for modernization. It helps them to acquire all social skills for leading a better future life. And better future life accelerates the process of modernisation. Therefore, it is a powerful weapon that can accelerate the pace of modernisation in the present society for a happier and salubrious life.

Modernization of Education in India: Problems

The path of modernization of education in India may be paved with many difficulties. India is marching on the path of economic development within the framework of a free and democratic society and therefore it cannot adopt authoritarian means to modernize education. Firstly, the centre needs to get the consent of the states and each state has to get the same from its elected representatives in their legislative assemblies before introducing any major change in the allocation of resources for introducing changes in educational system . Secondly, India is as yet a developing nation, with limited resources, which are directed primarily to meet the basic needs of its huge population. But,it can avail assistance from advanced and prosperous countries and international agencies like UNESCO which have specially developed programmes to assist educational development in developing countries. However, the fact that this aid may not be sufficient should be taken into account. Thirdly, India is a land of diversities. India has mixed economy, where modern means of production and modern practices co exist with traditional and orthodox and even outdated practices and beliefs, and at many places. The same is true of thoughts and value-system as well as life styles of its citizens. The tribal, rural and urban groups in India show extremely wide contrasts in their physical and social conditions of living. Such extreme varieties and contrasts in society pose a great challenge in formulating and implementing a uniform system and curricula in the sphere of education. The aims, methods and objectives of education which may be beneficial for one group may be worthless for the other; and vice versa. Lastly, in Western societies, economic development and modernization preceded political and social modernization. Consequently, in their educational planning and development, they could lay more emphasis on the needs of the individual than on the economic needs of the country. But India, being largely agricultural and monetarily challenged, to a great extent, has to put the economic needs of the country at the fore before it can embark on a journey to social and individual development, which is brought about only through education. Hence in a country like India, the majority of resources and capital cannot be spent with a free hand on new and innovative and expensive educational programmers that are not productive in realizing immediate economic gains. Thus, the Indian education system needs a complete overhaul through proper legislation and its effective implementation. Legislations should be made taking into account the regional diversities, advances in technology as well as cultural and social temperament of each state. The masses should be made aware of the new developments, their accessibility, their utility and benefits.1

Education and Modernization in India:

To the common man industrialization and automation symbolise modernisation. In machine he sees, on the one hand, increased production resulting in better comfort and higher standard of living and, on the other hand, science displacing superstition.

In education also, modernisation implies many things. To one educationist modernisation means to spread education, to produce educated and skilled citizens and train an adequate and competent intelligentsia. To another it implies more teaching aids to make teaching-learning effective. A comprehensive view of modernisation in education will mean a new approach not only to the aims and processes of education but also to the totality of its entire programmers to relate it to national development, national needs and national aspirations.

Contemporary education, which is an agent of modernization in various forms, is also of the Western origin. Traditionally, content of education was esoteric and metaphysical; its communication was limited to the upper classes or the 'twice-born' castes and the structure of its professional organization was hereditary and closed.

The roles both teachers and the taught were qualitative-astrictive. Modern education has a fundamentally different orientation and organization. Its content is liberal and exoteric, and it is steeped in modern scientific world-view. Freedom, equality, humanism and denial of faith in dogmas are the themes which a modern education should contain. It has a professional structure which is not ascribed to any specific group or class but can be achieved by merit by any one in society. Some branches of modern education such as science, engineering and medicine directly focus on a world-view which embodies the core values of modernization, and imparts skill to realize the goal of a modern society. Traditional Indian education departed fundamentally from these normative and organizational prerequisites.

The foundation of modern education in India was established by the British. Its historical landmarks are: Macaulay's policy of 1835 to promote European learning through English, Sir Charles wood's dispatch of 1854 which for the first time recognized the need for mass education with the private and missionary help and gave up the policy of selective education known as the 'filtration theory', and finally the first Indian Education Commission of 1882 which recommended the initiative of private Indian agencies in the expansion of education.

Gradually, a broad structure of educational organization emerged in India which may be roughly classified into three groups: first, primary- vernacular education (except for the English missionary schools); secondly, high school and secondary school education and, thirdly, college and university education.

From the very beginning a contradiction between the primary and the college-university level of education emerged in India because of the medium and content of education. At the primary level the medium of instruction (except for missionary and public schools) was the regional language and at the college level it was English.

Teaching of science and European literature was done at the colleges and universities to which select few had access; but the mass education at the primary level remained isolated from this main current. This lag in the structure of education which started from the time of Macaulay has still not been fully bridged. Modernization through education thus right from the beginning in India has been confined to a sub-culture of college and university educated youth and elite and never did become a mass phenomenon.

In the expansion of education, too, in early days there was more emphasis on the higher education than primary education. In the nineteenth century the rush was for higher education, specially, among the urban middle classes and the growth in higher education was also considerable.

Primary education was neglected till education became a provincial subject. For instance, "the number of scholars in all kinds of colleges in 1921 was 59,595. It rose to 144,904 in 1939, nearly 2.4 times as much. The number of pupils in schools of all kinds during the same period increased from 8.32 to 14.55 million, only 1.7 times as much. The difference in the pace of college and school education was accentuated in the decade following 1939. In 1949-50, for example, the number of all kinds of college students rose to 380,837, is, 2.7 times as much in ten years. The corresponding figure for pupils in all kinds of schools rose from 14-55 23.66 million, an increase of only 1.6 times as much. Higher education was thus becoming increasingly top heavy, especially after British influence". The school population now stands at about 50,000,000 and the literacy rate is nearing 25 per cent. This aspect of the expansion in education has contributed to many important sociological problems in cultural change in India.

The significance of education in modernization could be analysed in three areas: first, the cultural content of this education, secondly, its organizational structure and thirdly, the rate of its growth. The content of new education was doubtlessly modernizing and liberal in nature.

This is true whether reference is made to the humanities or social science or natural and applied sciences. The literary content of the courses in the humanities and social sciences was drawn from the literature of the European Renaissance, Reformation and Enlightenment. Its themes were humanistic, secular and liberal. An important element in this education was emphasis on contemporaneity and humanistic evaluation of social, political and historical issues. Its sociological result was disenchantment from traditional education, whose categories being embedded in the scriptural and mythological lore's had an obsessive degree of orientation towards the past. The categorical structure of the new education was oriented to the present and the future. Disciplines like history, geography, political science and economics, etc., in the curricula had a subtle orientation to focus the attention of students on social and physical realities and on the world- view of contemporaneity and anthropocentrism. This it marked a major break from the traditional outlook and system of values.

In cultural modernization through education often more positive value is associated with learning of physical and biological sciences, medicine and engineering rather than the humanities and social sciences. The reason for this association is not only that science education has more modernizing effect than arts, but because this education creates manpower which is indispensable for economic and industrial growth.Nevertheless, if the creation of a substantial profession in science and engineering contributes to modernization of society, education in the humanities and social sciences contributes to the modernization of man. Every individual is unique with respect to his or her tendencies and potentialities so, one must not be considered less significant than the other.

The idols of the Victorian generation, which in India lived longer than they did in the West, continue to hold high places mainly because they continue to be 'set books' in secondary schools, and colleges. Apart from the emphasis on the works of Western thinkers and litterateurs a current of cultural introspection and new look on traditional literature was simultaneously going on in India. Its symbols were drawn from the pragmatism of the Vedas, the logical metaphysics of the Upanishads and the karma yoga or the philosophy of positive action as contained in the Gita.

Leaders like Vivekananda, Tilak, Gokhale, Gandhi, and Aurobindo established the foundation of this tradition. A militant nationalist culture flourished in Bengal, Punjab, Maharashtra and some other parts of India. This cultural process served to counterbalance the effect of Western education and its literary and cognitive content. The new education was also different in its organizational structure. It was impacted by teachers who were appointed based on educational achievement irrespective of their caste or birth, a principle which was in basic contrast with the concept of Guru (teacher) in the Hindu tradition who had to be a Brahmin by caste.

Not only the content of education but also the structure of the teaching profession was thus secularized. Training schemes for teachers in the primary, middle and high and higher-secondary schools were launched. In Bengal, first

Normal School for teachers was established in 1844 and the district primary and middle school education was placed under the charge of Inspector of Schools.

The Education Code of 1904 for the first time made the appointment of a certain minimum number of trained teachers a necessary condition for the recognition of schools. During 1919-20 the total number of vernacular teachers in India was only 201,000, of which 70,000 were trained. The teachers in Anglo- vernacular schools during the same period were 100,000 of whom 35,000 were trained and 11,000 possessed a degree. Since then there has been a tremendous expansion in primary, middle and high school education. The total number of teachers in lower primary schools during 1950-51 was 537,918 of whom 82,281 were women. During the same year the number of teachers in higher primary schools was 85,494, about 12,887 of these being women.

The estimated number of lower primary school teachers by 1965-66 is about 1, 050,000; out of this 200,000 would be women. For the same year the number of higher primary school teachers is estimated to be 520,000, about 140,000 being women. Although the rate of growth in the number of teachers has been low, through this profession an organized pattern for cultural diffusion in the country has emerged which contributes to the Great tradition of modernization in India.

The expansion of primary and secondary levels of education has been followed by growth in higher education. To the three universities, Bombay, Calcutta and Madras which were established in 1857, fifteen more were added till the end of the British rule in India. After Independence, however, the number of universities has more than doubled. Between 1947-66, forty- six new universities have been established and nine Institutes have been deemed to be universities."

About 2,565 colleges are being controlled by the sixty-four universities which are functioning in India, with a total enrolment of 15, 28,227 students. Comparing it with the figures in 1911, when there were only 186 colleges and about 13,551 students (in graduate and post-graduate courses), the progress is phenomenal. Percentage increase in the output of post-graduate students in basic sciences has been of 120.6 per cent during 1950-51, of 83.6 per cent during 1955-60, and of 48.2 per cent during 1961-63. The number of engineering students, which during 1889-94 totalled only 1,104 (an average of about 221 students per annum) was recorded in 1964-65 alone to be 78,114. However, it may be added that as compared to the total number of students pursuing higher education, this number constitutes only 5.4 percent, which is small. However, the balance of enrolment between science and humanities (arts) has been considerably made even if we compare the 42.0 per cent of total enrolment of students for arts courses with 31.3 percent enrolled for science degrees and additional 12.4 percent enrolled for degrees in engineering, medicine, agriculture and veterinary science.

Progress has also been made in other spheres of educational planning and modernization of its organization. Percentage of girls going to schools and colleges has increased. In many States schooling of children has been made free and compulsory. New vocational and poly-technical institutions have been started for better utilization of educated manpower for the economic and social growth of the country. The working conditions and salaries of teachers at all levels have, been improved to a considerable extent, although some imbalances remain. But all this growth appears phenomenal only in temporal sense. In magnitude the growth rate of education does not seem to be very impressive or phenomenal. Also, the expansion of education has not led to a sociologically meaningful degree of social mobility and change in stratification system. Higher education is still primarily confined to the upper classes, is a scarce good and reflects the advantages of wealth and social origin More than seventy- five per cent of people is still illiterate. The proportion of national income devoted to education in India is small in comparison with educationally advanced countries of the world.

Despite these limitations, education has been one of the most influential instruments of modernization in India. It has led to the mobilization of people's aspirations for nationalism, liberalism and freedom. It alone has been responsible for the growth of an enlightened intelligentsia which carried forward not only a movement for Independence but also a relentless struggle for social and cultural reforms. It has created a sub-culture of students in India which though not fully modern, contains elements of transition from tradition to modernity. The persistent strains that we find in the internal system of this sub-culture partly reflects the stresses of transition from one constellation of values to another and partly results from the structural maladjustment of this culture with that of the larger society. Yet, its modernizing significance is self-evident.

Finally, the educational system has contributed to modernization by growth of new forms of rationally organized structures in the shape of school, colleges and universities, which serve as cultural networks for the diffusion of knowledge and cultural categories which are modem in ethos. However, some elements of conflict between tradition and modernity can persistently be discerned in the functioning and administration of the educational system in India at all levels. Whereas modernization has in some forms been welcomed there has also been a conscious effort to preserve the traditional values. This has a very logical explanation. Modernization in all traditional cultures goes along with the process of a new identity consciousness. Since the former is outer-directed process, the latter must necessarily be inner- directed. Hence identity consciousness finds its basic symbolic structure in the past tradition. Nationalism, as a modernizing process in such societies emerges as a queer blend of modern psychology of outer-directedness and the core commitment to tradition as revealed by inner-directed search for national symbols.

In the field of education, a good example is the following statement in the Report of the Education Commission, 1964-66, appointed by the Government of India:

"The most powerful tool in the process of modernization is education based on science and technology. The one great lesson of the present age of science is that with determination and willingness to put in hard work prosperity is within the reach of any nation which has a stable and progressive government. There is no doubt that in the years to come India's trade and commerce will grow; there will be more food for all; more education, better health and a reasonable standard of living will be available. But India's contribution can, and should be far more than these material gains. She should learn to harness science, but she must also learn not to be dominated by science."

Role of Education in the Modernisation of India:

* Education and Increased Production.
* Education and Equalisation of Educational Opportunity.
* Education and Promotion of Emotional and National Integration.
* Education and Establishment of a Socialistic Pattern of Society.
* Education for Democratic Values.
* Education and Secularism.
* Education for International Understanding.
* Education and Synthesis between Scientific and Cultural Values.

The following are the recommendations regarding the impact of modernization on programs of educational reconstruction suggested by the Education Commission (1964-66).

EXPLOSION OF KNOWLEDGE: During the last few years, there has been an explosion of knowledge. In the traditional society, the quantum of knowledge was limited, and the main aim of education was preservation, maintenance and promotion of the existing culture. But in the present society the quantum of knowledge is very vast. Knowledge earlier was received passively but now it is discovered actively. The traditional society believed in 'to know' but now the society believes in 'to know by heart', this leads to creative and critical thinking. The Education Commission also emphasis by observing the present condition to have better methods of teaching in the new concept of education and to have well training of teachers at the school and colleges level without much of boredom.

RAPID SOCIAL CHANGE: Due to the rapid social changes the education centres should be a step ahead in the teaching methods. There is need of a dynamic policy in the field of education. The Education Commission also believes that unlike the traditional methods of teaching, the teaching should bring awakening of mind, curiosity, development of interests, attitudes, values and building up essential skills. For example: to differentiate between good/bad and critical thinking and better judgement.

NEED FOR RAPID ADVANCE: Once the process of modernization has started we cannot step it in the half way to go back to the traditional society. Hence, there is need for a rapid advance to take this modernization to peaks. It is obvious to get problems, issues, like economical, cultural and political. But we need to overcome and move rapidly forward.

MODERNIZATION AND EDUCATIONAL PROGRESS: With regards to modernization and education progress the Education Commission too feels that the progress in modernization is proportional to the education. Modernization is a process of bringing change. Modernization does not necessarily mean a complete change in or isolation of own tradition.

For modernization attempts should be made on foundation of the past, reflecting the needs of the present and vision for the future. Modernization of the Indian society should be based on morals and spiritual values and self-discipline. Education Commission also believes that modernization will lead towards offering individual a larger way of life and wider variety of choices. Freedom of choice has some advantage no doubt, but it is also dependent on the value system and motivation. Knowledge and power of individuals gets expanded and individuals develop a deep sense of social responsibility and power of appreciation of moral values and spiritual values. Modernization should not be madly followed at the cost of human values. Therefore, attempts should be made in to inculcate value oriented education at all the stages of education. Children should learn to maintain a balance between spiritual and material values of life while modernizing them.

To modernize the Indian society, we have few problems that include:

- Problems of mass-illeteracy.
- Socio-political problems.
- Modernization brings changes in the social structure, values and social norms.
- Problems of National Integration.
- Problems of Science and technological development etc.

CHAPTER FOUR

Education and Culture

Culture is believed the centre of any society and without it, no society can even exist. Horton and Hunt defines, "Culture is everything which is socially shared and learned by the members of a society." Culture is a fundamental concept in anthropology and sociology, encircling the range of phenomena that are transmitted through social learning in human societies. Some definations of culture are as;

According to E.A. Hoebel, "Culture is the sum total of integrated learned behaviour patterns which are characteristics of the members of a society and which are therefore not the result of biological inheritance." The modern term "culture" is based on a term used by the Ancient Roman orator Cicero in his Tusculanae Disputationes, where he wrote a cultivation of the soul or "cultura animi," using an agricultural metaphor for the development of a philosophical soul, understood in teleological aspect as the uppermost possible model for human development.

Philosopher Edward S. Casey (1986) describes: "The very word culture meant 'place tilled' in Middle English, and the same word goes back to Latin colere, 'to inhabit, care for, till, worship' and cultus, 'A cult, especially a religious one.' To be cultural, to have a culture, is to inhabit a place sufficiently intensive to cultivate it—to be responsible for it, to respond to it, to attend to it caringly.

Meaning of Culture

In anthropological text the term culture is used in different senses, but in general writing it is used to indicate social behavior, customs, beliefs, norms and intellectual dominance.

Culture is a combined term for socially transmitted behavior patterns.

In normal language culture means the customs, ideas, and social behaviour of a particular people or society.

Taylor defines culture as "that complex whole which includes knowledge, belief, art, morals, and law, custom and any other capabilities and habits, acquired by man as a component of society."

Ellwood says that "culture includes man's entire material civilization, tools, weapons, clothing, shelter, machines and even system of industry."

According to Brown, "both material and non-material are dependent upon each other".

Culture is the customary beliefs, social forms, and material traits of a racial, religious, or social group.

The culture of a group is the way of life of that group like- the things they value, the things they do not value, their habits of life, their work of art, what they do, what they like etc.

Types of Culture

Material culture includes all the resources and physical objects that people of the particular society uses to define their culture. For example clothes, machines, industry, factories and plants, means of production, goods and products, and so forth.

Non material culture includes all those nonphysical ideas, attitudes and values that people have about their culture, including beliefs, values, religion, norms, morals, language and organizations. For example, the religion consists of a set of ideas and beliefs about God, worship, morals, and ethics.

Characteristics of Culture

- Culture is sum total of all acquired traits.

- Culture is learned, shared, based on symbols, integrated, and dynamic.
- Culture is Continually Changing.
- Culture is transmissive as it is transmitted from generation to generation through theprocess of communication and interaction.
- Culture is Idealistic as it embodies the ideas and norms of a group. .
- Culture is cumulative.
- Culture is adaptive.
- Culture is pervasive as it touches every aspect of life.
- Culture is the products of behaviour.
- Culture changes and nurtures with the time.
- Culture is abstract. It exists in the minds or habits of the members of society and is the shared ways of doing and thinking.
- Cultural traits and patterns are transmitted from generation to generation.
- Culture is dynamic rather static

Education and Culture

? Cultural and education are interdependent that cannot be separated from each other.

? A society free from any culture will have no definite educational organization.

? The culture of a nation has a very influential impact on its educational patterns.

? It is the culture in which education develops and flourishes as a result exerts a nourishing influence.

? Education as a part of culture has the double functions of conservation and modification of the culture.

? Education is envisaged as a systematic attempt to maintain a culture. In other words, "In its technical context, education is the process by which society, through its educational spaces like schools, colleges, universities and other institutions, purposely transmit its cultural heritage, its accumulated knowledge, values and skills from one generation to another."

? Education is considered as an instrument for cultural change.

? One of the main aims of education is to impart a child his cultural and social heritage.

? Every individual is born into a particular culture that provides him with specific patterns of behavior and values then guide his/her conduct in different situations of life.

Major Functions of Culture

Adaptation to the natural environment

? All over the world humans live in a specific natural environment to which they adapt themselves without this adaptation he cannot survive.

? The differences in natural environment of different communities pave the way for differences in their cultures.

? It is this mode of behavior that makes up culture. Adaptation to the social environment

? Culture includes customs, traditions, beliefs etc. and all of these helps an individual to adapt to his social environment.

? It must be conceived that all these elements undergo steady changes as there is change in social environment.

? Culture establishes the patterns of social control, through which the individual is subjected to remain attached to that group.

? The advantage in communicating the culture of the group to the child by the means of education is that he/she is thereby familiar with the traditions, customs, values and patterns of conduct existing in his group.

? Therefore this information enables him to adapt to social environment and thus achieve his socialization.

Development of personality

? The personality of the individual is perceptible through his pattern of behavior.

? Culture influences the physical, mental, moral, social, aesthetic and emotional aspects of individual.

? The behavior of the individual is greatly influenced by the culture

School as a Community in Miniature

? School is a social institution that has been established by the society for the function of conveying those ideas, beliefs, attitudes and dispositions that will make them valuablemembers of the society.

? The school is to be thought not as a place where conventional knowledge is transmitted as authoritative but as a place where experiments in life are carried on.

Culture and Education

Culture and education are two inseparable parameters and they are interdependent. Any educational pattern gets its guidance from the cultural patterns of a society. For instance, in a society with a spiritual pattern of culture, the educational focus would be on the achievement of moral and eternal values of life. On the contrary, if the culture of a society is materialistic, then its educational pattern will be shaped for the attainment of materialistic values and comforts. A society which does not follow any culture definitely has no definite educational organization. So, the culture of a country has a very powerful impact on its educational system.

Today while human lives continue to live in local realities, the lives and experiences of youth growing up will be allied to, social processes, economic realities, technological and media innovations, and cultural flows that go across international borders with ever greater momentum. These worldwide transformations will involve youth to adapt to new skills that are well ahead of what most educational systems can now distribute.

Culture should be regarded as the set of distinctive spiritual, material, intellectual and emotional features of society or a social group, and encompasses, in addition to art and literature, lifestyles, ways of living together, value systems, traditions and beliefs. Culture shapes individual's worldviews and the way communities address the changes and challenges of their societies. For this reason, education serves as a critical vehicle for transmitting these value systems as well as for learning from the humanity's diversity of worldviews, and for inspiring future creativity and innovation. (The Culturalization of Human Rights Law, Federico Lenzerini,2014)

The most powerful and influential method to solve any social and economic issues in the society is nothing but, learning through cultural engagement at all levels and for diverse target groups. There is an urge and special consideration on the cultural sector in educational and lifelong learning programs as it has been ignored as the positive impact at all levels is indisputable.

The roles of educational institutions, educators, and educational materials in a cultural formation and transformation are for the overall growth of a human being.We learns about the social and cultural values through education. Education makes students ready to deal with cultural ethics and norms. There are many materials and educational sites, which the focuses on culture development of education. Individual's adoption of natural and social environment in a positive way takes place via cultural elements. Each person of the society has his or her own preference and mentality to perceive the world around. Education changes the perception of the individual toward different forms of community.

Education seems to be a foundation of the transmission, and at times, the transformation of culture. Understanding this interaction is complex, in part because "education" and "culture" are difficult to portray with precision; and in part because the interaction goes in both directions: culture has an impact on education along with, great impact of education on culture. Education has the privilege, authority and potential to reshape the process of thinking of the society and culture across the globe. J.L. Nehru viewed, "Education must help in preserving the vital elements of our heritage".

Culture plays a vital role in every individual's life. It brings together numerous elements to create a unique way of living for different people. Some of the major elements that exist in every culture and many change with time as the society progresses are symbols, language, values, and religion. The first element is variety of symbols. A symbolis used to stand for something. People who share a same culture attach a specific denotation to an object, gesture, sound, or image. For instance, Christians use a cross as a significant symbol to the religion. It is not just two pieces of wood attached to each other, nor is it just an old object of torture and execution. To Christians, it represents the basis of their whole religion, and they have great respect for the symbol.

The second factor in every culture is a language. Languageis a structure of words and symbols used to communicate with other community. Beside English, Spanish, French there are other unique languages which belong to certain groups of people. Those are slang, common phrases and body language. For example, English is most common and fluent spoken language in America and Britain, however, we see and hear slangs and phrases that mean different things; American cookies are British biscuits; American French fries are British chips, and so on.

A system of value is a culture which is defined for standard what is good or pleasant. There is a share system of values which is used by member of the cultures to evaluate what is right and what is wrong. In West, people are individualistic, they strongly believe in competition and emphasize on individual achievement. According to the culture whoever gets promotion is appreciated for his/her hard work and talent. However, in East the collectivist values of culture are in oppose to the West. In East there is a strong believe on welcoming the collaboration and an individual's achievement is only as good as his/her contribution to the group.

Last but not least, religion in any culture is a unique phenomenon. Religion is still important in global societies, in twenty first century, and in each country since communities of worship can provide not only great chances for emotional and spiritual development but also a system of support to public in all phases of their lives. This sense of belonging is crucial for human happiness.

Influence of Education on Culture

Impact of Education on Culture:

Just as the culture influences education, in the same way education also influences culture of a country. It can be seen in the following manner:

1 Preservation of culture:

2. Transmission of culture: '

3. Development of culture:

4. Equips Man to Adapt to Changing Cultural Patterns:

5. Development of personality:

1. Preservation of Culture:

Every country has a distinct culture of its own. Hence, it tries to preserve its culture and its distinctiveness in its original form. Education is the only means through which this task can be accomplished. Thus, education preserves the culture of a society.Culture is the blood vein of a society, which needs to be conserved. It is an important function of education to help in the preservation of culture or social heritage.

Education, through its specialized agencies, tries to inculcate the traditions, customs, values, arts, morals etc. into the tender minds of pupils.

T.P. Nunn has emphasized this aspect in his views on education. Our first prime minister, Pt. J.L. Nehru viewed, "Education must help in preserving the vital elements of our heritage".

2. Transmission of Culture:

In addition to preservation of culture, it is a task of education to maintain the continuity of culture by handing down the existing cultural experiences, values, traditions, customs etc. from one generation to another through its various programmes and practices. Without this transmission, the nation's survival may be the toughest task and the progress of mankind can be stifled. Society reels in utter chaos and confusion.The process of preservation includes the process of transmission from one generation to another. The famous sociologist Ottaway has rightly remarked 'The function of

education is to transmit social values and ideals to the young and capable members of the society.

Men will become savages and human relationship will be broken into pieces. Therefore, the substance of unity in any society is its precious culture. The famous sociologist, Ottaway writes, "The function of education is to transmit the social values and ideals to the young and capable members of society".

3. Promotion of Culture:

Besides preservation and transmission, another vital function of education is to modify the existing cultural patterns in the light of changes visible in the needs and demands of the society. These changes are heightened owing to cross-cultural variables. Thus, new cultural patterns are formed by replacing and reorienting the old outmoded cultural forms to suit the changing needs of time and man. Therefore, society makes ostensible progress. This part of education is called progressive function of education. As such, education performs by constantly reorganizing and reconstructing human experiences for the promotion and enrichment of culture.The function of education is to bring the needed and desirable change in the cultural ideals and values for the progress and continued development of the society without which social progress can not take place. Education accultures an individual modifiescultural processes by research and deeper investigations into all areas of human requirements.

4. Equips Man to Adapt to Changing Cultural Patterns:

It is an admitted fact that every generation after generation modifies the old and archaic cultural forms and adds new ones to the best advantage of theirs. This is possible through educational means and method. Moreover, education equips the individual to adjust himself or herself to the changing cultural forms and patterns for better and successful living.

5. Moulding the Personality:

It is an universal element of culture that personality is shaped and moulded by education. An individual's personality goes on developing when he or she continues to forge a web of relationship with other members of society.Education aims at developing the personality of a child. It employs diverse cultural patterns of thinking, behaviour and cultural values so that children are physically, mentally, morally, socially and intellectually develop with the development of society to the
maximum extent.

This form of interaction is made possible by education according to the behavioural patterns or culture of the existing society. In simple words, culture is an informal agency of social control which helps in moulding and shaping the behaviour of the individuals in a desirable way.

6. Restoring Unity of Mankind through Diffusion of Culture:

It is a dire necessity of the civilization that unity of mankind is to be restored. It is to be made possible through education which assists in diffusion of culture in an effective manner. Education should treat human culture as a whole like a full-bloosom flower whose different petals represent different groups.

Education, further, helps in disseminating the modern cultural values like co-operation, unity, mutual understanding, brotherhood of men, love and appreciation for others etc. to the mankind for its enduring survival.

7. Removing Cultural Lag:

The concept of cultural lag is attributed to the famous sociologist Ogburn. When there exists a difference between material culture and non-material culture, there emerges this lag concept. As it is seen, material culture is advanced due to the rapid strides in science and technology and people adopt the modern life styles ignoring non-material part of culture.

Therefore, non-material culture lags behind the former. This situation is cultural lag which needs to be eliminated by education through its various programmes and myriad activities. Cultural is antithesis to social change and progress of the civilization.

8. Continuity of culture: Culture is a life breadth of a society. Without which a society is bound to decay. Education upholds the continuity of culture through its diverse activities and programmes.
A society establishes schools to preserve and transmit its culture to the coming generations. Children should be motivated to learn more and more from cultural interaction among various cultures. Thus cultural integration and assimilation will enrich the composite culture of a society.

From the foregoing discussion, it is crystal clear that there exists a close relation between education and culture. Education socializes an individual in one hand and it preserves, transmits and promotes the culture of a society on the other. In brief, education and culture are mutually interwoven, complementary and supplementary in all their aspects. It is education which reifies the culture.

Culture is an umbrella term which includes all the material and non-material aspect of any human society. Culture consists of the derivatives of experience, more or less organized, learned or created by the individuals of a population, including those images or encodements and their interpretations (meanings) transmitted from past generations, from contemporaries, or formed by individuals themselves.' (T.Schwartz 1992; cited by Avruch 1998: 17). Therefore, we may culture is a social mirror and is always in dynamic change.

Impact of Culture on Education

The aims and ideals of the education are influenced by the values and patterns of the society.

1. Curriculum: The curriculum is prepared according to the culture of society. The system of education tries to realize the cultural needs of society through curriculum which conditions all educational activities and programmes.

2. Methods of teaching: Culture and methods of teaching are intimately connected. The changing cultural patterns of a society exert its influence upon the methods of teaching. Previously teaching was teacher centered where teacher used to give knowledge to the child. Now it has become student centered. The teacher considers the needs, interests, aptitude, attitude, inclinations, behaviour etc before teaching. In this way education is a method of preparing child for the future for effective living. In short we can say that cultural and social conditions generate the methods and techniques of teaching in a powerful manner.

3. Discipline: Cultural values influence the concept of discipline. The present cultural patterns of thinking and living are directly linked to our concept of discipline where the democratic values are accepted all over the world.

4. Text Books: Curriculum is contained in the textbooks. Textbooks are written according to the formulated or determined curriculum. Only those textbooks are welcomed which foster and promote cultural values and ideals.

5. Teacher: Each individual teacher is imbibed with the cultural values and ideals of the society of which he/she happens to be an integral member. Only such teacher achieves his/her missions successfully. They infuse higher ideals and moral values in children.

6. School: A schools is a miniature of a society. The total activities and programmes of a school are organized according to the cultural ideals and values of the society which establishes and organize the school. Hence, school is the centre of promoting, moulding, reforming, and developing the cultural pattern of the society.

7. Culturally responsive Pedagogy:

Culturally responsive pedagogy is a student-centered approach to teaching in which the students' unique cultural strengths are identified and nurtured to promote student achievement and a sense of well-being about the student's cultural place in the world. Culturally responsive pedagogy is divided into three functional dimensions: the institutional dimension, the personal dimension, and the instructional dimension.

The institutional dimension of culturally responsive pedagogy emphasizes the need for reform of the cultural factors affecting the organization of schools, school policies and procedures (including allocation of funds and resources), and community involvement. The personal dimension refers to the process by which teachers learn to become culturally responsive. The instructional dimension refers to practices and challenges associated with implementing cultural responsiveness in the classroom.

CHAPTER FIVE

Diversity in Society

Understanding Indian Society with reference to diversities

What is diversity meaning?

Diversity refers to the reality created by individuals and groups with the concept of acceptance and respect.

'Diversity' means collective differences among people, that is, those differences which mark off one group of people from another. These differences may be of any sort: biological, religious, linguistic etc.

On the basis of biological differences, for example, we have racial diversity. On the basis of religious differences, similarly, we have religious diversity. The point to note is that diversity refers to collective differences.

It is based on the spectrum of demographic and philosophical differences.

Diversity can also be alongside the dimensions of ethnicity, race, gender, socio-economic status, sexual orientation, physical abilities, age, political beliefs, religious beliefs, or other ideologies.

In simple terms, it is the degree or measure of differences in identifying features. The features are similar among the defined group.

The term diversity is opposite of uniformity. So when there is something common to all the people, we say they show uniformity. When students of a school, members of the police or the army wear the same type of dress, we say they are in 'uniform'.

Like diversity, thus, uniformity is also a collective concept. When a group of people share a similar characteristic, be it language or religion or anything else, it shows uniformity in that respect. But when we have groups of people hailing from different races, religions and cultures, they represent diversity. Thus, diversity means variety.

However, diversity needs to be differentiated from fragmentation. Diversity means existence of differences in a whole. It does not mean separate parts. Fragmentation does not mean differences, it means different parts and in that situation each part would be a whole in itself.

For all practical purposes it means variety of groups and cultures. We have such a variety in abundance in India. We have here a variety of races, of religions, of languages, of castes and of cultures. For the same reason India is known for its socio-cultural diversity.

India is a land of "Unity in diversity". The high mountain ranges, vast seas , large river-irrigated lands, countless rivers and streams, dark forests, sandy deserts, all these have adorned India with an exceptional diversity. Among the people there are numerous races, castes, creeds, religions and languages.

The term "Unity in diversity" refers to the state of togetherness or oneness in-spite of presence of immense diversity. "Unity in diversity" is based on the concept where the individual or social differences in physical attributes, skin colour, castes, creed, cultural and religious practices, etc. are not looked upon as a conflict. Rather, these differences are looked upon as varieties that enrich the society and the nation as a whole.

Unity in diversity is a very important principle because we all live in a diverse world and it is crucial to respect each other and to support each other no matter what our culture, background, gender, orientation or other differences may be.

In India, there are a large number of ancient culture prevailing or still practicing today. Though there are several numbers of diverse cultures in India, still it has unity in diversity.

The modern Indian civilization has been nourished and developed by multiracial contributions. From times immemorial, diverse races migrated into India by via land and sea routes and get themselves settled here. In course of time they are absolutely absorbed in India's social life.

The ancient ethno-linguistic groups, such as, the Aryans, the Austrics, the Negritos the Dravidians, the Alpines and the Mongoloids, had combined to constitute the modern Indian race.

In the historical period, diverse branches of the aforementioned unique ethnic groups – the Persians, the Pallavas, the Kushanas, the Greeks, the Sakas, the Huns, the Portuguese, the Arabs, the Turks, the English and the European races came to India, and enriched Indian ethnicity and culture by their contribution to the same.

The Indian people composed of several racial elements have a range of languages among them. Official accounts confirm that more than two hundred languages are present in this country. Each region has its own language. The local people speak in their own language. In spite of the fact that there are numerous languages among various races, there is a sense of national unity and oneness among all the Indians. It is this spirit of patriotism that binds us together as one nation.

India is a plural society both in letter and spirit. It is rightly characterized by its unity and diversity. A grand synthesis of cultures, religions and languages of the people belonging to different castes and communities has upheld its unity and cohesiveness despite multiple foreign invasions. National unity and integrity have been maintained even through sharp economic and social inequalities have obstructed the emergence of egalitarian social relations. It is this synthesis which has made India a unique mosque of cultures. Thus, India present seemingly multicultural situation within in the framework of a single integrated cultural whole. The term 'diversity' emphasizes differences rather than inequalities. It means collective differences, that is, differences which mark off one group of people from another. These differences may be of any sort: biological, religious, linguistic etc. Thus, diversity means variety of races, of religions, of languages, of castes and of cultures. Unity means integration. It is a social psychological condition. It connotes a sense of one-ness, a sense of we-ness. It stands for the bonds, which hold the members of a society together. Unity in diversity essentially means "unity without uniformity" and "diversity without fragmentation". It is based on the notion that diversity enriches human interaction. When we say that India is a nation of great cultural diversity, we mean that there are many different types of social groups and communities living here. These are communities defined by cultural markers such as language, religion, sect, race or caste.

'Diversity' is the assortment of people who bring a variety of backgrounds, styles and beliefs as assets to the groups and organizations which they interact with. 'Diversity' is any collective mixture characterized by complexities, similarities and related tensions and differences. It means valuing thedifferences between people and the ways in which those differences can contribute to a richer, more creative and more productive working environment. Diversity includes understanding that each individual is unique, and recognizes our individual differences. These can be along the extent of age, ethnicity, gender, physical abilities, political beliefs, sexual orientation, socio-economic status, race, religious beliefs, or other ideologies. The concept of diversity includes acceptance and respect. It is the examination of these differences in a harmless, positive, and cherishing environment. It is about moving beyond humble tolerance, to celebrating and embracing the rich magnitudes of diversity bounded within each individual and understanding each other.

Diversity includes keeping an open mind to differences among cultures, perspectives and people. It means recognizing, valuing and taking account of the differences in people's backgrounds, experiences, knowledge, needs and skills. It is also about encouraging those differences and using them to create a cohesive community and effective workforce. There are various kinds of diversity, such as linguistic, cultural, architectural, religious, political, social, regional, etc. Some of these shall be discussed here in detail.

Linguistic Diversity (Linguism)

Concept and Characteristics of Linguistic Diversity

India is a multilingual society in which there is no common language linking the entire nation together. The language problems have been perplexing the minds of our National Leaders considerably even before the attainment of Independence. Language is a rich and powerful vehicle of expression creating a sense of unity among the people speaking it. In India, states have been organised on the basis of languages. "One state, One language" is the universal feature of almost every state. It is right to say that one language can unite people, while two languages are sure to divide people. We feel close and protected when we talk to a person who speaks our mother tongue rather than a person who speaks other languages. Thus language can either unite or differentiate people. This differentiation can give rise to social conflicts. Therefore, an attempt was made by the government to make Hindi the principle official language of India in 1965. Linguistic States

1. Formation of the States Reorganisation Commission by the Government of India. (after Independence)

2. Recommendation of the division of the country into a number of states, 14 big states and 6 centrally administered areas.

3. This division met the wishes of some linguistic groups.

4. The groups which could not get their demand fulfilled began to agitate. Linguistic riots occurred at many places.

5. The movement by those interested in the division of the states yielded fruits.

6. This gave an impetus to the movements for carving out new states from the old ones. Thus, the division of the country on linguistic basis has been very much responsible for the encouragement of the disruptive elements. These disruptive elements tried their best to create hatred among the people of different states.

Diversity of Languages Linguism may be defined as the consciousness or the loyalty of the people speaking a common language in a particular area. Linguism is the most formidable obstacle in the path of national unity. On 26th Jan. 1965, Hindi would have automatically become the National language but for the continuance of English as official language, simultaneously with Hindi. The agitation by the students in Tamil Nadu was misguided in its belief that Hindi was being thrust upon them. The cry of some demonstrators was to make English the language of the administration law courts in short to give it a National status. The language which is foreign, which is understood by hardly 2% of our people was sought to be thrust on 98% of the population. This was compounded by the fact that 70% of the population did not even know how to read or write in their own mother tongue. The language controversy is still very much present, though the violent agitations have been curbed. This controversy is disintegrating the nation. The South cries "Down with the Hindi imperialism".While the Hindi speaking section has a slogan, "Boycott English language anywhere and everywhere". If we wish to achieve national unity then the problem regarding a national language has to be swiftly settled. Language problem has never been as intensely felt as it is being felt today. Examples of Linguistic Diversity In Belgaum, there is a power struggle between the Marathi and Kannada speaking people. Assam was similarly challenged with Bengali and Assamese language conflict. Although Hindi has been recognized as the national language, this has promoted bitter hostilities, predominantly in the South. Even Bihar and Uttar Pradesh are not free from the linguistic problems. Further, conflict tends to persist among the Urdu, Hindi and Oriya linguistic groups and Urdu and Hindi speaking people respectively.

Causes of Linguistic Diversity

1. Psychological causes: People belonging to a particular region are attached to that region's language which is also their mother tongue. Hence, they do not easily consent to learn another Indian language. Language has certain characteristics, both psychological and emotional, which invoke the feeling of ethnocentrism to a homogeneous group. In India, the linguistic groups are tied together by a binding common interest. This creates a spirit of sectarianism, regionalism and a separatist feeling in the mind of the inhabitants.

2. Historical causes: In the past, numerous foreign countries had invaded India. The French invaded Pondicherry and established their supremacy, as did the Portuguese in Goa. Mughals, during their rule brought Persian language to India. The British brought with them the English language to India. As a result, Indian languages became subject to the control or the authority of these languages. This gave birth to linguism, as the people from different regions promoted their own regional language in the states that they conquered and ruled in.

3. Geographical causes: Every language has its own literature. Literature is influenced everywhere by local geographical conditions such as plains, mountains, local vegetation and culture. It reflects the life of the people who speak the language. Therefore, an individual does not readily accept it if the language of another region is forced upon him/her. Geographical conditions tend to promote linguism. People living in a particular locality mostly speak the same language. This promotes a unified sense of local identity and distinctiveness among the people. Living together geographically reinforces a linguistic group's love for their own language.

4. Economic causes: Amongst the causes of linguism are economic causes. The government sometimes provides financial assistance for the progress of some languages, but people speaking other languages object to this. This gives rise to linguism.

5. Political causes: Linguism is also inspired by the political interests and aspirations of different politicians and political groups. During election in order to win votes many political parties raise the language issue to instigate their people and win their votes. Parochial politics creates a feeling of linguistic divisiveness among the people of a locality and exploits their sentiments. 6. Social causes: Linguism is encouraged by some social factors-e.g. Selection of National Language. The language that is approved by the society is respected by all. In contrast, the languages that cater to contradictory presumptions are objected. This leads to linguism. E.g. South Indian states like Tamil Nadu insist on the continuance of English as the Associate official language along with Hindi.

Regional Diversity (Regionalism)

Concept and Characteristics of Regional Diversity

Regionalism has always been present in India in one form or the other but never has it risen to such magnitude as it does today and neither was it ever as detrimental to any national interest as it is in the present context. Originally the Indian states that were formed after Independence, were princely states. Today the states are based on linguistic patterns. Right after Independence there were some large states such as Bombay Presidency, Madras Presidency etc. Bombay state was rather large and was split into Maharashtra and Gujarat in 1960. Similarly, the Punjab state was split into Punjab and Haryana in 1966. In 1963 the state of Nagaland was formed. Subsequently in 1972 Manipur, Meghalaya and Tripura were formed. In 1987 Arunachal Pradesh and Mizoram were formed and In 1971 Himachal Pradesh was formed. More recently states like Uttarahand and Telangana have been formed based on linguistic and regional considerstions.

Regionalism is the narrow selfish tendency of people to think only in terms of regional interest. Regionalism is the sense of affection and attachment towards people belonging to one's own region and hatred for those who belong to some other regions. As a result of this, people of one region in India have started looking at people from some other part of the country as foreigners. They want only the people of their own area to run the government in their region, and they refuse to make any place for people who have migrated from some other region; irrespective of the period for which they may have been living there. In this way some people have demanded the formation of a separate state of Nagaland in the Naga area.

The Akali party of Punjab has demanded the formation of a Punjab Sabha. It was on the basis of region that the state of Bombay was divided into two separate states, those of Gujarat and Maharashtra. In addition, the politicians belonging to certain parties along with few people with vested interests are demanding that the south should be formed into an entirely separate unit. Regionalism may be defined as consciousness and loyalty to a distinct area within a country, usually characterized by common culture and language or historical and social background. Loyalty to a particular region to which one belongs is of course very natural and not necessarily a negative force.Regionalism is nothing but a concept of a region. A region may be defined as a well-defined territorial unit including in particular a language or ethnic group or tribe, having particular social setting and cultural pattern like folk dance, music, folk art etc. Each region has a distinct socio-cultural personality within the territorial frame-work of India. Regional loyalty to a particular region assumes a dangerous form for national unity, when regional loyalty overrides all other national considerations and becomes the sole guiding principle. Examples of Regional Diversity

1. Clashes between the people:

(a) The border dispute i.e. which part is in Maharashtra and in Karnataka (Belgaum) e.g. Kaveri river.

(b) The high court of Punjab and Chandigarh was contested wherein, Chandigarh was a union territory. 2. River water dispute:

(a) Kaveri River starts in Karnataka and flows to Tamil Nadu (b) The dam Bhakra Nangal in Punjab which stopped water for the lower states.

3. (Power) Electricity disputes: These include disputes over where the electricity is generated from. Causes of Regional Diversity There are many causes at the root of Regionalism in the country, the major ones being the following:

1. Geographical cause: The main cause of Regionalism is geographical. There is some essential difference between food habits, language, life, etc. of every region and people who live there. By virtue of these differences they come to regard each other as foreigners and they acquire an attitude of fear and hatred towards each other. People living in different geographical areas get adapted to the climatic conditions of that region. Hence they find it difficult to adjust to them when they move to a different region.

2. Historical cause: There have been some differences between people of the North and South ever since the time of the Aryans and these have continued. Many of the kings of the North have won over the South, while there have been few kingdoms in the South which have extended to the Northern part of India. For this reason many South Indians look upon Northern India as separate from Southern India.

3. Political cause: If the situation is carefully and minutely observed, it will be seen that the main causes at the root of regionalism present in the country are of a political nature. Many politicians have demanded the formation of regional government and in this they have been inspired by regional interests and by the aim of gaining power. In this direction a major part has been played by the revolutionary Naga party, the Akali party of Punjab, the D.M.K party of South India and other political parties. They are responsible for having propagated regionalism in these respective areas. Some representatives of different areas who are members of political parties give prime importance to the interest of their own regions even in the face of national interests.

4. Psychological causes: People often desire their area to progress the most. This idea in itself is neither bad nor detestable, but when this is done at the cost of the national interest and those of other regions then the feeling takes on the form of regionalism. (It is expressed by hatred, jealousy, fear, anger etc.)

5. Marital and Economic cause: As a general rule people belonging to different regions do not inter-marry and hence the occasion for close contact between the two does not arise. In addition to this there are some economic causes of regional tension. In the country there are some regions that are far more backward in comparison to other regions. As a result there often arises a sense of inferiority and jealousy among the regions. The people of Marwar, Gujarat and Punjab are seen to be particularly successful businessmen and they have a practical monopoly in the sphere. Due to this they are hated by some people who try to turn them out from their own regions. Religious Diversity (Communalism) Concept and Characteristics of Religious Diversity Communalism is an ideology which states that society is divided into religious communities, where the interests differ and at times are even opposed to each other. The hostility practiced by the people of one community against the people of other religion and community can be termed as "Communalism". This often results in communal tensions. Moreover, in democracies, the political parties exploit these communal ideas and foster them to secure their selfish interest. Communalism, thus, is a severe threat to the harmony and secular spirit of a country. It implies an extreme sense of pride in and identification with one's own (religions) community to the extent of being antagonistic towards another community.

Hindu-Muslim clashes and the conflicts between Hindus and Sikhs arise out of mutual antagonism between these religious communities. That is why such clashes are termed as communal conflicts. Communalism carries negative implications like riots, terrorism, and destruction of public property, raping and killing of women thus creating a feeling of insecurity. Communal violence creates fear and terror. Communalism follows no law and order. A Communalist is a person who is essentially interested in using and exploiting religion for some personal/private/ political purpose with the sole object of gaining power, position, status, influence, wealth and cheap publicity. The outcome of communalism may be positive as well as negative. The negative aspect is already discussed. The positive outcome, for example is the Parsee community providing generous scholarships for the people of their community. There is some reason (common cause) why these acts take place. For example, if it is something related to a taxi then all taxi men will go on a strike to raise the price, out of a sense of kinship and shared cause. Communalism leads to violence as it is based on mutual religious hatred. This phenomenon leads to distinction between a communal organization and a religious organization. Communalism essentially has following main features:

1. It is based on orthodoxy and intolerance.

2. It is exclusive in outlook. A communalist considers his own religion to be superior to other religions.

3. It also propagates intense dislike of other religions. It stands for elimination of other religions and its values and it adopts extremist tactics including use of violence against other people.

Causes of Religious Diversity (Communalism)

1. The British policy of Divide and Rule: British imperialism deliberately promoted communalism for the purpose of sowing dissension in the minds of the major religious communities i.e. the Hindus, Muslims, Sikhs, Christians, Parsis, etc. by systematically following the policy of divide and rule in order to perpetuate British rule in India.

2. Socio-Economic changes: In our tradition bound society, socio-economic changes that took place after Independence caused a sense of insecurity among the members of the society (directly affected by them) organisations like VHP, RSS, etc. fully exploit religion to promote their electoral, political or private interests. Economic disparity and inequality are causes of communalism.

3. Role of Anti-Social Elements of the Underworld: These elements operate mostly in urban areas. They deal in illicit liquor and drugs, smuggling of foreign goods and illicit arms. They play a pivotal role in communal conflicts and riots. The criminalization of politics and politicization of crime with money and muscle power of the underworld contribute to communal riots.

4. Selfish Vested Interests: Political parties and government use religion and tradition as diverting tactics after failing to fulfil the expectations of people. Some parties tell the religious minorities that they are being discriminated against by majority dominated governments.

5. Unemployed Youth: The energies of frustrated, educated, unemployed or under employed youth, are particularly targeted to keep them busy in divisive politics. Youth in India today has fallen prey to communal leadership. 6. Religious factor: The religious factors include decline in norms and secular values, use of religion for political gains, communal ideology of religious leaders propagating narrow and dogmatic religious values. Social factors include social traditions and customs, caste and class ego as well as inequality.

7. Orthodoxy and Obscurantism: A feeling of being a separate entity with their own personal laws, thought and cultural pattern is felt by the orthodox members of religious minorities. There are strong elements of fundamentalism and conservatism among the Muslims. The concept of religious tolerance and secularism has not been accepted by them due to such feelings.

8. Design of the Leaders: Communalist leaders desire to nurture the communally divisive tendencies of both Hindu and Muslim communities to propagate and achieve their own agendas. This has led to the thriving of communalism in India. The demand for the organization of Muslim league before independence and a separate electorate were the practical indicators of this line of thought. The British rule which produced the divide and rule policy i.e. separate electorate on the basis of religion, strengthened the basis of communalism in India ultimately, the antagonistic feeling towards each other was further intensified by the partition of the country into India and Pakistan.

9. Weak Economic Status: A majority of Muslims in India have failed to adopt technological and scientific education. They have not been represented sufficiently in the public service, industry, trade, etc. due to their educational backwardness. This causes the feeling of relative deprivation, thus sowing the seeds of communalism.

10. Social Causes: Cultural similarity is a powerful factor in encouraging cordial relations between any two social groups. But the social customs, institutions and practices of Hindus and Muslims are so different that they think themselves to be two distinct communities.

11. Psychological Causes: Psychological factors are an important factor in the development of communalism. The Hindus think that the Muslims are fundamentalists and fanatics. They also believe the Muslims to be unpatriotic. On the contrary, the Muslims feel that they are being treated as second rate citizens in India and their practices and religious beliefs are seen as inferior. These feelings cause an ill-feeling instead of communal harmony.

12. Provocation of Enemy Countries: Some foreign countries try to destabilize our country by setting one community against the other through their agents. Pakistan has played a role in fostering communal feeling among the Muslims of our country. Pakistan has been promoting and encouraging communal riots by instigating the militant sections of the Indian Muslim community. To destabilize India's internal security by spreading communal venom, the Kashmir youths are trained by Pakistan. 13. Negative Impact of Mass Media: Through mass media the messages

relating to communal tension or riot in any part of the country are spread. This results in further riots and tension between two rival religious groups.

Examples of Religious Diversity (Communalism)

Anti-Sikh riots, 1984 - This was one of the most bloody incidents in Indian history, where Sikhs in large numbers were massacred by an anti-Sikh mobs. This massacre took place in response to the assassination of Prime Minister Indira Gandhi by her own Sikh bodyguard in reaction to her actions authorising the military operation into the most holy temple of the Sihs-the Golden Temple to flush out the terrorists. **Ethnic cleansing of Kashmiri Hindu Pundits in 1989 -** Kashmir is known as the heaven of India and was known for its Kashmiryat, i.e. the reflection of love, peace and harmony through brotherhood as well as the unity of Hindus, Muslims and other communities living together. However, due to Extremist Islamic terrorism in the Kashmir valley the brotherhood was dealt with a serious blow, which led to mass killings and large scale exodus of Kashmiri Pundits from the valley to the various regions and corners of the India. This ended up giving them the status of refugees in their own country. Since then the on-going unrest has become a problem for the development of these people and the valley is in the grip of communal violence. **Babri masjid demolition in Ayodhya, 1992 -** According to Hindu mythology, Ayodhya is the birth place of Lord Rama and therefore it is a sacred place for the Hindu religion. But in the medieval period Mughal general Mir Baqi, built a mosque there, named after the Mughal ruler Babur. Thus began the disputes and the riots, which have continued. In 1990 there was atmosphere of protest by Hindu religious groups, due to political mobilisation. On a large scale "karsevaks" visited Ayodhya from all parts of India, in support of demolishing Babri masjid and building Ram temple in its place. These movements caused a huge amount of bloodshed and since then it has become a disputed matter. After this, more violence was followed by the Godhra incident in 2002, when "karsevaks" in a Sabarmati Express, returning from Ayodhya were killed by a fire in the coaches of the train. This act was followed by the prolonged communal violence in Gujarat. That very violence has become a black spot in the history of Gujarat and the nation too, as people were killed without any mercy. Hindu and Muslim communities have become antagonistic towards each other. Even now people are fighting for justice in the Supreme Court.

Assam Communal violence, 2012 - North eastern states are known for their distinctive tribal population and ethnic diversity. Large scale Bangladeshi immigration has changed the demography of North eastern states, which often becomes a reason for clashes. In 2012, there were clashes of ethnics between Bodos (Tribal, Christian and Hindu faith) and Muslims. Ethnic tensions between Bodos and Bengali-speaking Muslims spiralled into a riot in Kokrajhar in July 2012, when four Bodo youths were killed by unidentified miscreants at Joypur.

Muzaffarnagar violence, 2013 - The cause of this ethnic clash between Jat and Muslim community in the Muzaffarnagar district of Uttar Pradesh is very much disputed and has various versions. Some claim, it started after some suspicious post on the social media platform (Facebook). According to some, it only escalated after the eve teasing case that took place in Shamli. Whatever the reason may be, greater importance can be accorded to the nature and large scale loss to the country with respect to human resources and peace.

Linguistic, Regional and Religious Diversity Challenges of Linguistic Diversity

1. Increasing Regionalism and Parochialism: The people of different linguistic groups belonging to a particular state seem to only think of the interests of their own States. This causes parochial feelings and undermines consideration of national issues.

2. Formation of Regional Political Parties: Linguism has given rise to regionalism which has eventually led to, in some states, the formation of regional political parties. Some of these parties have also formed a government. Such political parties in power end up complicating the Centre-State relationship.

3. Persecution of the Linguistic Minorities: The safeguarding of linguistic minorities existing in the states has been provided by the State Reorganization Commission. However in reality, the linguistic minorities are being harassed in different States. As a result disturbing trends and certain complications have developed which seem to threaten the unity of the country.

4. Demand for Separate States: Due to selfish motives of politicians linguistic conflicts take place. These politicians, for their own gain, instigate the minorities to demand partition of the States along linguistic lines. These demands for a separate state create problems for the centre as well as the concerned state.

5. **Threat to National Integration:** The feeling of national integration is eroded due to regional and linguistic loyalties. The sovereignty of the country is threatened by the erosion of the national feeling.

6. **Inter-State Border Dispute:** In the border areas which tend to be bilingual, language problems have created tensions. For example, the people of Goa are divided on the basis of Konkani and Marathi languages.

Challenges of Regionalism

1. Lack of national integration: People belonging to the same region cling to each other. They give preference to their region or state rather than the country. They give more importance to region than their nation. For example, North Indians are affected with regional prejudice against all South Indians.

2. It hinders the nation's progress: Due to regionalism there is unrest in the areas. No communication takes place. There are no trade transactions resulting in depletion of resource (man and material), hindering the nation's progress.

3. Inter-state rivalry competition: In cases where there is sharing of water, electricity and the location of the state and central projects there is rivalry among the concerned states. Similarly, certain regions are given preferential treatment when it comes to allocation of funds for development. For example, Each railway minister wants to improve the train service in their own region.

4. Son of soil movement: The people belonging to a particular state of region have the right to claim every privilege of the state. This is demanding preferential treatment for local residents to the point of exclusion of all outsiders. For example , Assamese against Biharis, Shiv Sena against Biharis.

5. Social disintegration: The social values deteriorate, people don't mingle and socialize resulting in social disintegration. 6. Problem of internal security in the nation: Example, Khalistan movement by Sikhs a few years ago demanding for a separate state of their own.

7. Mistrust and suspicion: It leads to insecurity, hatred, jealousy, anger and eventually leads to violence which in turn leads to destruction of life and property. Some other effects are - Regional biases prevent social progress, give rise to nepotism, regional prejudice in social life, housing, marriage, social interaction and narrow group loyalties.

Challenges of Religious Diversity (Communalism)

1. Communal riots lead to heavy destruction, increase in unemployment, acute poverty, segregation of different communities, poverty, slums, etc. The minority groups suffer tremendously; the losses are physical, emotional, psychological social and hence irreparable. It exhausts the country's resources and cripples it.

2. Religious diversity leads to communal violence and riots. It also leads to disruption of life and property. This in turn causes individual and social disorganization and ultimately threatens national integration. Near and dear ones are lost. People lose faith in the law and order and even faith in a friend of different community.

3. Religious diversity causes fear, suspicion, hatred, insecurity in the minds of the victims. Communal riots lead to heavy destruction, increased unemployment, acute poverty and segregation of different communities.

4. Religious diversity affects the poor classes, slums and minority groups tremendously. It also produces widows, orphans, who are homeless and destitute.

5. Religious diversity exhausts the resources of the country and cripples the economy of the country. Religious diversity leads to separation and fragmentation of the nation into small parts that can never be put together

Role of Education: Linguistic, Regional and Religious Diversity Education is the common unifying factor that can bring about change in the dividing factors of the country on a large scale. It is being made available everywhere in the country and can thus be utilized to bring together and strengthen the unity of our nation.

Various forms of diversity in India:

Religious diversity: India is a land of multiple religions. Apart from the tribal societies, many of whom still live in the pre-religious state of animism and magic, The Hindus themselves are divided into several sects such as Vaishnavas, Shaivates, Shaktas, Smartas etc. Similarly, the Muslims are divided into sects such as Shias, Sunnis, Ahmadiyas etc.According to the data on Population by Religious Communities of Census 2011, Hindu 96.63 crores (79.8%); Muslim 17.22 crores (14.2%); Christian 2.78 crores (2.3%); Sikh 2.08 crores (1.7%); Buddhist 0.84 crores (0.7%); Jain 0.45 crores (0.4%) are dispersed all over the nation forming cultural pockets.

Linguistic diversity: Languages spoken in India belong to several language families, the major ones being the Indo-Aryan languages spoken by 75% of Indians and the Dravidian languages spoken by 20% of Indians. Other languages belong to the Austroasiatic, Sino- Tibetan, Tai-Kadai, and a few other minor language families and isolates. India has the world's second highest number of languages, after Papua New Guinea. Racial diversity: 1931 census classified India's racial diversity in the following groups- The Negrito, The Proto-Australoid, The Mongoloid, The Mediterranean, The Western Brachycephals and the Nordic. Representatives of all the three major races of the world, namely Caucasoid, Mongoloid, and Negroid, are found in the country.

The relationship between language and culture is perfectly embedded. In fact they are entangled. Peoples Linguistic Survey of India identified 780 languages of which 50 got extinct in past five decades. Officially there are 122 languages but 22 languages in the Eighth Schedule of the constitution give cultural pockets like Assamese, Gujarati, Konkani, Maithili, Manipuri, Oriya, Tamil, Telugu etc.

Racial diversity:

The dictionary by Merriam-Webster defines race as "a category of humankind that shares certain distinctive physical traits."

Race is usually associated with biology and linked with physical characteristics, such as hair texture or skin color and covers a relatively narrow range of options. Yet people of similar complexions/hair textures can be defined as different races, and definitions in the United States have changed over time.

While some may be considered to be of a certain race, Black for example, people may identify more with their individual ethnicity, as opposed to race. This could apply for any member of any race.

Race consists of the following categories:

- White
- Black or African American
- Asian
- American Indian or Alaska Native
- Native Hawaiian or Pacific Islander

Most contemporary anthropologists categorize Indians as belonging to racial admixture. Mongoloids are largely confined to the North-eastern region whereas Negritos are found on the Andaman Islands.

Ethnic diversity:

Ethnicity is a broader term than race. The term is used to categorize groups of people according to their cultural expression and identification.

Commonalities such as racial, national, tribal, religious, linguistic, or cultural origin may be used to describe someone's ethnicity.

While someone may say their race is "Black," their ethnicity might be Italian, or someone may say their race is "White," and their ethnicity is Irish.

As per the 1901 census, the eight different ethnic groups found in India are: 1. Pre-Dravidian 2. Dravidian 3. Indo-Aryan 4.Turko-Iranian 5.Scytho-Dravidian 6. Arya- Dravidian 7. Mongoloid 8.Mongoloid-Dravidian. Because of this, India has been termed as an ethnological museum. A particular ethnic group shared a common culture, common language or dialect, a common religion, a common norm, practices, customs and history. Such multiple groups appeared as cultural pockets.

Caste diversity: India is a country of castes. The term caste has been used to refer to both varna as well as jati. Varna is the four-fold division of society according to functional differentiation. Thus, the four varnas include Brahmins, Kshatriyas, Vaishyas and Shudras and an outcaste group. Whereas Jati refers to a hereditary endogamous status group practicing a specific traditional occupation.. There are more than 3000 jatis and there is no one all India system of ranking them in order and status. The jati system is not static and there is mobility in the system, through which jatis have changed their position over years. This system of upward mobility has been termed as "Sanskritization" by M. N. Srinivas.

Cultural diversity: Cultural patterns reflect regional variations. Because of population diversity, there is immense variety in Indian culture as it is a blend of various cultures. Different religion, castes, regions follow their own tradition and culture. Thus, there is variation in art, architecture, dance forms, theatre forms, music etc.

Geographical diversity: Spanning across an area of 3.28 million square kilometre, India is a vast country with great diversity of physical features like dry deserts, evergreen forests, lofty mountains, perennial and non-perennial river systems, long coasts and fertile plains.

In addition to the above described major forms of diversity, India also has diversity of many other types like that of settlement patterns – tribal, rural, urban; marriage and kinship patterns along religious and regional lines and so on.

Factors Leading to Unity Amidst Diversity in India

Constitutional Identity

The entire country is governed by one single Constitution. Even, most of the states follow a generalized scheme of 3-tier government structure, thus imparting uniformity in national governance framework. Further, the Constitution guarantees certain fundamental rights to all citizens regardless of their age, gender, class, caste, religion, etc.

Religious co-existence:

Religion tolerance is the unique feature of religions in India due to which multiple religions co-exist in India. Freedom of religion and religious practice is guaranteed by the Constitution itself. Moreover, there is no state religion and all religions are given equal preference by the state.

Inter-State mobility:

The Constitution guarantees freedom to move throughout the territory of India under Article 19 (1) (d), thus promoting a sense of unity and brotherhood among the masses. Other factors such as uniform pattern of law, penal code, and administrative works (eg. All India services) too lead to uniformity in the criminal justice system, policy implementation etc.

Economic integration:

The Constitution of India secures the freedom of Trade, Commerce and Intercourse within the Territory of India under Article 301. Further, the Goods and Service Tax(GST) have paved way for 'one country, one tax, one national market', thus facilitating unity among different regions.

Institution of pilgrimage and religious practices:

In India, religion and spirituality have great significance. From Badrinath and Kedarnath in the north to Rameshwaram in the south, Jagannath Puri in the east to Dwaraka in the west the religious shrines and holy rivers are spread throughout the length and breadth of the country. Closely related to them is the age-old culture of pilgrimage, which has always moved people to various parts of the country and fostered in them a sense of geo-cultural unity.

Fairs and festivals:

They also act as integrating factors as people from all parts of the country celebrate them as per their own local customs. Eg. Diwali is celebrated throughout by Hindus in the country; similarly Id and Christmas are celebrated by Muslims and Christians, respectively. Celebration of inter-religious festivals is also seen in India.

Climatic integration via monsoon:

The flora and fauna in the entire Indian subcontinent, agricultural practices, life of people, including their festivities revolve around the monsoon season in India.

Sports and Cinema:

These are followed by millions in the country, thus, acting as a binding force across the length and breadth of India.

Factors that threaten India's unity:

Regionalism:

Regionalism tends to highlight interests of a particular region/regions over national interests. It can also adversely impact national integration. Law and order situation is hampered due to regional demands and ensuing agitation.

Divisive politics:

Sometimes, ascriptive identities such as caste, religion etc. are evoked by politicians in order to garner votes. This type of divisive politics can result in violence, feeling of mistrust and suspicion among minorities.

Development imbalance:

Uneven pattern of socio-economic development, inadequate economic policies and consequent economic disparities can lead to backwardness of a region. Consequently, this can result in violence, kick start waves of migration and even accelerate demands of separatism.. For instance, due to economic backwardness of the North East region, several instances of separatist demands and secessionist tendencies have sprung up in the region.

Ethnic differentiation and nativism:

Ethnic differentiation has often led to clashes between different ethnic groups especially due to factors such as job competition, limited resources, threat to identity etc. E.g. frequent clashes between Bodos and Bengali speaking Muslims in Assam. This has been accentuated by son of the soil doctrine, which ties people to their place of birth and confers some benefits, rights, roles and responsibilities on them, which may not apply to others.

Geographical isolation:

Geographical isolation too can lead to identity issues and separatist demands. The North-East is geographically isolated from the rest of the country as it is connected with the rest of the country by a narrow corridor i.e the Siliguri corridor . The region has inadequate infrastructure, is more backward economically as compared to the rest of the country. As a result, it has witnessed several instances of separatism and cross-border terrorism, among others.

Inter-religious conflicts:

Inter-religious conflicts not only hamper relations between two communities by spreading fear and mistrust but also hinder the secular fabric of the country.

Inter-state conflicts:

This can lead emergence of feelings related to regionalism. It can also affect trade and communications between conflicting states. For instance, Cauvery river dispute between Karnataka and Tamil Nadu.

Sometimes external factors such as foreign organizations terrorist groups, extremist groups can incite violence and sow feelings of separatism. E.g. Inter-Services Intelligence (ISI) has been accused of supporting and training mujahideen to fight in Jammu and Kashmir and sow separatist tendencies among resident groups. In-spite of the challenges posed by diversity, there can be no doubt on the role played by sociocultural diversity in sustaining and developing Indian society.

Problem is not of diversity per se, but the handling of diversity in India society. The problems of regionalism, communalism, ethnic conflicts etc. have arisen because the fruits of development haven't been distributed equally or the cultures of some groups haven't been accorded due recognition.

CHAPTER SIX

Inequality

Inequality

The United Nations describes inequality as "the state of not being equal, especially in status, rights and opportunities".

Inequality can be broadly classified in to:

Economic inequality: Economic inequality is the unequal distribution of income and opportunity between individuals or different groups in society.

Social inequality: It occurs when resources in a given society are distributed unevenly based on norms of a society that creates specific patterns along lines of socially defined categories e.g. religion, kinship, prestige, race, caste, ethnicity, gender etc. have different access to resources of power, prestige and wealth depending on the norms of a society.

Both these categories are deeply intertwined and inequality of one type affects the inequality in another e.g. Social Inequality due to gender have large impact on income of women. In patriarchal societies large gender wage gap tends to exist.

"All of us do not have equal talent, but all of us should have an equal opportunity to develop our talent." This has been rightly said by the former U.S. President John F. Kennedy.

Social inequality means inequality that exists due to factors like gender, caste, race, religion, or financial position which devoids a person from equal opportunities and rewards in society. People are not equal on economic and social terms. There can be many factors which can lead to social inequality like societal factors, custom, or poverty.

Social inequality has been prevalent in India for a long time. Various measures were undertaken to reduce these inequalities. There are various provisions in the constitution as well as statutes that aim to reduce inequality in Indian society. Still, the rank of India in the global mobility index indicates inequality that still persists in the country. There are various types of social inequalities existing in India like gender inequality, deprivations, etc. Some of the major inequalities are-

Regional disparity increased in the 1990s with southern and western parts doing better than northern or eastern parts. The economic disparity also increased within states.

The most persistent inequality in India is in the income and distribution of income and resources among the people. This is due to factors like family influence and inheritance etc.

There exists a large scale difference between people employed in the formal and non-formal sector. People received less money in the informal sector when compared to formal sectors.

There have been inequalities faced by various communities in the country. This has often led to various conflicts within groups or between one social group and the other.

People are still fighting on the basis of religion. There exists inequality between these groups on various fronts like employment and education. For instance, upper-caste Sikhs and Christians are more affluent than upper-caste Hindus in both urban and rural areas.

The caste system followed in India has been abolished but only on paper. People still practice the same. There exist wide inequalities between upper caste people and lower caste people.

India is facing social inequality in the country in the present scenario as well. The government took various steps like reservations for special groups. However, these steps have not worked to a great extent. Instead, it has led to more conflicts among the communities. Even various land reforms and wealth redistribution could not help in eliminating the existing income inequality in the country.

India is a country with numerous castes, religions, languages, beliefs, cultures, status, etc. The people of India are different from each other in several aspects such as economic, social, cultural, religious, etc. The major reason for the disparity amongst the people arises because of the distinction in economic status between them. It is usually observed that in India people with a different language, religion, or caste can live in a society together if their economic status is equal. India being a welfare state should focus on equitable growth in the economy but in reality, it is observed that there has always been inequality in the distribution of wealth and income.

This inequality in the distribution in turn leads to social and economic distress as well. It is necessary for the overall development of the country that economic inequality be reduced and eventually removed. For such reduction and removal, the Indian government has taken several steps such as the five-year plans but the inequality instead of reducing has taken a turn to increase and widen over time.

Rise in inequality

After the introduction of early reforms in the early 1990s, India achieved unprecedented per capita growth rates but this growth was also accompanied by rising inequality, a severe issue of concern. The rise of inequality has been observed to increase between 1983-2012. Although poverty has fallen and many have escaped from it still, they are at high risk of falling back into that category. Moreover, those who are still in poverty, suffer from very severe problems, with continuous deterioration in their situation and hence, even any helping hand by the government through the introduction and expansion of safety nets cannot reach them.

A study on income inequality, based on the combination of multiple data sources and novel techniques, (Chancel and Picketty, 2017) suggested that income inequality in India declined sharply between the 1950s to 1980s but it went on to increase thereafter. During the 1980s it reached 10% and then thereafter it has been increasing rapidly. The estimates of income inequality place India as the country with the highest rate of inequality, internationally. The Gini index is an indicator of inequality. It varies from zero, which refers to perfect equality, to one, which refers to complete inequality. The Gini coefficient for wealth based on The All India Debt and Investment Surveys (AIDIS) rose from 0.67 in 2002 to 0.83 in 2017, putting India among countries with high inequality.

India's condition has improved and gained a better position at health and education over the past few decades, but it is not uniform. There are differences in levels of inequalities across social groups, states, and rural-urban areas. It reflects inequalities in the opportunity to access basic services.

Dimensions of inequality

In India, there are several dimensions in which inequalities are distributed. Inequality is an issue that cannot be described and discussed in a single context, rather it is subjected to various dimensions that have different reasons and different consequences. Broadly, inequality can be segmented into the following dimensions:

Local-level inequality

It is within rural villages and urban blocks. It accounts for the bulk of overall inequality in India. Its level varies considerably across the Indian states.

Social groups inequality

Inequality due to caste is one of the major categories for discrimination and inequality. Scheduled Castes and Scheduled Tribes are the ones who suffer the most due to caste discrimination. They are subjected to inequalities almost everywhere and their situation is worse across health, education, and monetary indicators.

People in India SCs and STs are still considered untouchables and they are allotted works such as sewage cleaners, etc. Although many Acts and provisions are enacted to reduce discrimination on caste still, there are many places where untouchability is being practised and people of low caste are subjected to do such jobs that are inhuman. The Untouchability (Offences) Act was introduced to punish the practice of untouchability and bring a uniform atmosphere where no person is treated unequally due to its caste.

Gender-based inequality

Women suffer a lot due to gender biases. Earlier women were not even educated as it was considered that they are born only for doing household works that require no education. Now the condition is better but still, they are facing continuous inequalities in jobs, nutrition, and education. Although now women are getting an education as the right to education has become a fundamental right. Women used to get low wages than men and even after working equally and working for equal hours. Article 39(d) of the Indian Constitution provides for equal pay for equal work and Article 41 provides for the right to work to all irrespective of their gender.

Women suffer from all sorts of harassment at the workplace. Many incidents and first hand accounts of rape, harassment, etc are reported frequently. The guidelines given by Supreme Court in the Vishakha case paved a way for the enactment of the Sexual Harassment of women at workplace (Prevention, Protection, and Redressal) Act, 2013. The Act came into force since 2013 but still, the awareness regarding the consequences of sexual harassment and its redressal is limited.

Status-based inequality

Those who are poor are subjected to inequality everywhere. Since they cannot afford much and they are not educated enough, people of better status and education misuse and take advantage of the poor. Children from villages move to cities for jobs and a better lifestyle where they are exploited by not paying them, making them do dangerous and life-risking tasks, making them servants, etc. The ones on or below the poverty line have to struggle for their mere existence as they do not have bread to feed themselves.

Monetary inequality

Monetary inequality can be divided into three aspects: consumption, income, and wealth. Consumption and income is a measurement of the flow of resources over time. Wealth refers to a stock of resources available at a point in time. The ratio between the richest and poorest deciles suggests that between 1993-1994 and 2004-2005 there was rising inequality and it continued to rise thereafter. In 2011-2012, the richest 20% of the population of the country accounted for 45% of the consumption.

The India Human Development Surveys (IHDS) is a nationally representative household panel survey. It collects comprehensive information on consumption and income. It indicates that income inequality in India was about 0.54 during 2004-2005 and 2011-2012.

An estimate of wage earnings was done by Rodgers and Soundararajan (2015) indicates an increase between 1993-1994 and 2004-2005. The Gini coefficient between 2004-05 for income inequality in India was almost 14 points higher than for expenditure.

Non-monetary inequality

Non-monetary inequality includes services such as health and education. These places also suffer a considerable amount of inequalities on the basis of caste, status, and gender. The National University of Educational Planning and Administration (NUEPA) in its annual report 2015 observed that from 1991 to 2013 there had been an increase by more than seven years in life expectancy at birth. The infant mortality rate fell by half, the maternal mortality ratio fell by about 60%, and the total fertility rate fell to almost replacement level. The report also observed that the education system has also expanded rapidly. The gross enrolment ratios had become 100 and 95 in primary and upper-primary classes respectively.

Dimensions of Inequality in India

In India, following are distinctive forms of social inequality:

Gender:

The Global Gender Gap Report, 2018, ranks India at 142 among 149 countries.

Four parameters for measuring gender inequality are economic participation and opportunity, health and survival, educational attainment and political empowerment.

Gender wage gap is highest in India according International Labor Organization women are paid 34% less than men.

Women comprise over 42 per cent of the agricultural labour force in the country, yet they own less than 2 percent of its farm land according to the India Human Development Survey (IHDS).

Caste

Caste is significant factor for determining access to resources like education, income, health valued by individuals.

India's upper caste households earned nearly 47% more than the national average annual household income, the top 10% within these castes owned 60% of the wealth within the group in 2012, as per the World Inequality Database.

Religion

Religious identities are significant for an individual's ability to mobilize resources.

Religious identities can cause prejudices which may lead to economic exclusion and other forms of discrimination which can impact jobs and livelihood opportunities.

While minorities such as Christians, Parsis and Jains have a larger share of income/consumption than their population share, Muslim and Buddhist populations have significantly lower access to economic resources.

Ethnicity

Tribal communities in India have been identified as ethnic group on the basis of their unique culture, language, dialect, geographical location, customs etc.

The National Family Health Survey 2015-16 (NFHS-4) showed that 45.9% of ST population were in the lowest wealth bracket as compared to 26.6% of SC population, 18.3% of OBCs, 9.7% of other castes.

Economic Inequality

The 2019 report by Oxfam, titled "Public good or Private Wealth?" showed that India's top 10% holds 77.4% of the total national wealth, while the top 1% holds 51.53% of the wealth.

The bottom 60% population holds only 4.8% of the national wealth.

13.6 crore Indians, who make up the poorest 10% of the country, have continued to remain in debt for the past 15 years.

The Gini coefficient of wealth in India in 2017 is at 0.83, which puts India among the countries with highest inequality countries.

Consequences of Inequalities

After many plans and programs initiated to reduce and remove inequality, still, there is no significant reduction in inequality and discrimination which is causing a great setback in the country. India is still considered to be a developing nation, the main reason behind it being the unequal distribution of money. People of lower castes belong to poor families and are mostly unemployed or work as daily wage earners that barely fetch them their bread for a living. Inequality due to the caste system is being practised all over the country which is detrimental for the country as the rich are getting richer and the poor getting poorer. India being a welfare county should focus on how the disparities get reduced and people obtain equal opportunities, services, jobs, status, and monetary distribution. Inequality is considerably dragging the country behind because people of the country also include the poverty-stricken people who are not developing due to which country will and is suffering.

Another consequence of rising inequality is that the Gini coefficient has been continuously increasing, placing India among the countries having the highest inequalities. Another consequence of inequality is the deteriorating situations of the poor. Government and its plans and programs are not fruitful and people who are placed below the poverty line are not being helped and supported.

Women empowerment is something that is heard whenever there happens any crime against women which raises the public's concern. In reality, plenty of crimes against women occur daily across the country. Women still are subjected to harassment and unequal payments. There is a requirement of creating an environment where women can speak up about their grievances without any fear of society and could get justice. There is also a need for sensitization of men towards the treatment of women at the workplace.

Rising inequality can affect political stability, the sustainability of economic growth, and the mobility of individuals. Growth and human development are determined by the existing state of income distribution. It is also dependent on the place of birth of an individual, his caste, community, religion, region, and gender. These factors affect an individual's access to opportunities, prejudice, marginalization, discrimination, or disadvantage. An individual's gender, caste, or community affects its participation in the labour market.

The dynamics of inequality has been seen to be different in different aspects. Somewhere it has been rising while in dimensions such as gender-based inequality, it has been observed that there has been a considerable decline in inequality as well. For the overall benefit of the population of the country, it is very essential to remove inequalities on any basis. Every individual should be treated equally and no one should be subjected to discrimination on any unreasonable ground. Article 14 and Article 15 of the Constitution of India provides for equality and prohibits discrimination. Discrimination and inequality are detrimental to the country but still, there is a continuous rise in inequality in the country. The state should make strict laws and regulations to reduce inequality. Proper legislation and for its execution, proper administration should be established so that inequality can be reduced in all its dimensions.

Inequalities tend to produce social conflict among the social groups e.g. caste groups like Jaats, Maratha, Patels are demanding reservations but this demand is opposed by caste groups already claiming the benefits of reservations, such clash of interest due to perceived inequality tend to produce violent conflicts between opposing caste groups.

Inequalities among ethnic groups have led to various ethnic movements demanding separate states or autonomous regions or even outright secession from India. North East has been rocked by numerous such ethnic movement e.g. by Nagas for greater Nagalim etc.

Religious inequality tends to generate feeling of exclusion among religious minority groups. This reduces their participation in mainstream, in India religious minorities have large population their economic exclusion compromises the GDP growth of nation as whole.

Poor development indicators like IMR, MMR, low per capita income, lower education and learning outcomes at schools, high rate of population growth can be traced to existing socio-economic inequalities.

High economic inequality is detrimental to public healthcare and education. Upper and Middle classes do not have vested interest in well functioning public healthcare and education as they have means to access private healthcare and education.

Factors of inequality

Differences across locations

It is an important source of rising inequality. The 2016-17 economic survey by the Department of Economic Affairs observed that eight low-income states, i.e., Assam, Bihar, Chhattisgarh, Jharkhand, Madhya Pradesh, Odisha, Rajasthan, and UP account for 50% of India's population still there occurs 71% of infant deaths, 72% of under-five mortality, and 60% of stunting. According to the Ministry of Health and Family Welfare and IIPS 2017, child stunting ranges from 2 in 10 children in Kerala, about 5 in 10 in UP and Bihar. The report also states that more than two-thirds of maternal deaths, and more than half of neonatal deaths occur in Bihar, Madhya Pradesh, Rajasthan, and UP.

Differences across social groups

The subsisting discrimination and distinction between SCs, STs, other backward castes (OBCs), and others is another factor paving the path for rising inequality. According to estimates based on NSS and IHDS data, the income and consumption share of SCs and STs are comparatively lower than the population shares. Meanwhile, OBCs are in a better position and have relatively higher shares than SCs and STs, but still, they have less share than population share. There is also a decline in income shares of the STs while there is an increase in the income share of others.

During the COVID-19 period, the daily wage workers had to and are still suffering the most, mainly because of no work to earn their bread. Their situation was so drastic that they had to return back to their villages barefooted. The return of the daily wage workers from Mumbai and other metro cities to their villages in Uttar Pradesh and Bihar was one of the most heart throbbing sights for every Indian. Their condition was proof of how financially weak they were, that they could not even afford to live without working for even a week.

An analysis by Chaudhary and Verick (2014) observed that between 2004 and 05 and 2011-12 when GDP grew at 8% per annum, the female labour force participation rate declined to 25% from 35%. The reason for this decline may be an increase in women's education, mechanization, and increasing formalization. Distinction based on religion is yet another reason. Minorities such as Christians do not have to suffer much discrimination but Muslims have to suffer more than even SCs and STs in urban areas.

Differences by occupation and factor ownership

A large section of the workforce is engaged in agriculture and employed in the unorganized sector. Unorganized sectors employ more workforce as compared to the well-paying sectors. Sectors such as finance, insurance, real-estate sectors, IT-related services, and telecommunications employ less than 2% of the workforce. Inequality among workers in the organized sector is a very small component of overall inequality still it emphasizes the changing nature of production. There is a rise in profit shares and a decline in gains to workers in the organized sector.

Measures to Deal with Inequalities

Constitutional Provision

Enforcement of Constitutional Guarantee of equality as enshrined in fundamental rights. Articles 14, 15 and 16 form part of a scheme of the Constitutional Right to Equality. Article 15 and 16 are incidents of guarantees of Equality, and gives effect to Article 14.

Promoting Civil Society

Provide a greater voice to traditionally oppressed and suppressed groups, including by enabling civil society groups like unions and association with in these groups.

Scheduled castes and Scheduled tribes should be motivated to become entrepreneurs, schemes like Stand up India need to be expanded to widen its reach by increasing funding.

Women Empowerment

For gender equality policies like affirmative action by reserving seats in legislatures, increasing reservation at Local self government both at Urban and village level to 50% in all states, strict implementation of The Equal Remuneration act,1976 to remove wage gap, making education curriculum gender sensitive, raising awareness about women right, changing social norms through schemes like Beti Bachao Beti Padhao etc.

Inclusion of Religious Minorities

Religious minority groups need special attention through representation in government jobs, provision of institutional credit, improvement of their education access, protection of their human rights by empowering National commission for Minority, strengthening rule of law etc.

Progressive Taxes

Additional public resources for public services by progressive taxes on wealthy more and by increasing the effective taxation on corporations, more importantly broadening the tax base through better monitoring of financial transactions.

Economic Policies

By ensuring universal access to public funded high quality services like Public health and education, social security benefits, employment guarantee schemes; inequality can be reduced to great extent.

Employment Generation

The failure to grow manufacturing sectors like Textile, Clothing, automobiles, consumer goods etc. is the important reason of rising inequalities.

The Labor-intensive manufacturing has the potential to absorb millions of people who are leaving farming while service sector tend to benefit majorly urban middle class.

India has committed to attaining the Sustainable Development Goals by 2030, and to end extreme poverty by that year.

According to Oxfam if India stops inequality from rising further, it could end extreme poverty for 90 million people by 2019. If it goes further and reduces inequality by 36%, it could virtually eliminate extreme poverty.

CHAPTER SEVEN

Discrimination and Marginalization

What is Social Discrimination?

Discrimination is treating different categories of people of a society or group in different manner that some categories among them are treated with injustice and prejudice by denying them privileges that are offered to the other categories because of some hidden causes

Discrimination may occur at two levels. They are

1. Individual
2. Social

Individual discrimination is when an individual is denied the provisions and rights give to others in a society on account of some prejudice. Individual discrimination occurs in families, in classrooms, and at times in society itself on account of prejudice of parents, lack of skill in classrooms, or because of some epidemic called aids.

Social discrimination occur when a particular group of a particular society is denied the provisions and rights given to other groups in that society on account of their existence in a particular gender, religion, cat, race, linguistic group etc. Here rights are denied not on the basis of one's individual traits or characteristics, but on the basis of the social background that he belongs to.

There are Different Types of Discrimination.

Gender discrimination or Gender bias is denying some particular gender groups the rights and opportunities that are enjoyed by some other gender groups of the same society only because they belong to this particular gender. Hence, if a person who belongs to a particular gender is denied an opportunity because that person doesn't deserve it on the basis of the qualifying criteria, it cannot be called gender discrimination or gender bias.

Racial discrimination is denying some particular racial groups the rights and opportunities that are enjoyed by some other racial groups of the same society only because they belong to this particular race. Hence, if a person who belongs to a particular race is denied an opportunity because that person doesn't deserve it on the basis of the qualifying criteria, it cannot be called racial discrimination.

Cast discrimination is denying some particular cast groups the rights and opportunities that are enjoyed by some other cast groups of the same society only because they belong to this particular cast. Hence, if a person who belongs to a particular cast is denied an opportunity because that person doesn't deserve it on the basis of the qualifying criteria, it cannot be called cast based discrimination.

Religious discrimination is denying some particular religious groups the rights and opportunities that are enjoyed by some other religious groups of the same society only because they belong to this particular religion. Hence, if a person who belongs to a particular religion is denied an opportunity because that person doesn't deserve it on the basis of the qualifying criteria, it cannot be called religious discrimination.

Linguistic discrimination is denying some particular Linguistic groups the rights and opportunities that are enjoyed by some other linguistic groups of the same society such getting education in their own mother tongue.

And it is widely said and discussed that there have been severe discriminations in India on the basis of religion, cast, race, language, gender etc., and for making such people, too, the part of mainstream, the Constitution as well as different Govt. policies offer some positive discrimination towards such people.

Positive Discrimination is some special privileges and reservation offered to the marginalized groups, in different developmental areas like education, employment, administration etc. to fetch them, too, into the mainstream of the society. It is also known as compensatory discrimination on the argument that they were marginalized on account of different historical and social factors

What is Marginalization?

Marginalization is forcing a person or a particular group of a particular society to be away from the mainstream of the society by denying him or it all the rights and opportunities for developing himself or itself by getting education and participating in such developmental activities

Social Exclusion is making a person or a particular group of a particular society out of the social order by denying them even the most primary human rights. It is a severe than marginalization that in marginalization, such groups enjoy the basic rights, though they are forced to remain at a corner of the society without getting opportunity for developing themselves, as the privileged groups do.It is clear that Marginalization and Social Exclusion Occur .

It is widely acknowledged that education has an important role to achieve a greater degree of social justice. The educational institutions are expected to equip children to the best of their ability for securing a meaningful place in society and thus fostering a process of developing an egalitarian society. However, a large number of children are still excluded from the educational system and hence cannot participate meaningfully in the economic, social, political and cultural life of their communities.

Concept of Marginalization The process by which a group of individuals is pushed to the margins of the society is called marginalization. It may be defined as a social process in which people are systematically blocked from opportunities, resources and rights. This leads to a stoppage of the individual members of a society from completely participating in the various aspects of the society that they live in, namely economic, social and political. Therefore, in this process some communities, groups, persons, or sections are able to enjoy opportunities and privileges while some are not. However these are meant to be enjoyed by all people as members of a particular society. The people denied are then pushed to a difficult state of powerlessness because of the disadvantage that arises due to their lack of participation in the economic, political and social spheres. They are expected to participate here but they are unable to do so. This group of people that are pushed to a marginal situation are referred to as a marginalized group. People are marginalized because of religion, culture, place of birth, caste, language and biological factors To clarify matters; marginalized as a term is used for those groups who have no access, or have a limited one to the economic, political, cultural and social spheres of society. The term therefore refers to something more than just oppressed and exploited. The term 'marginalization' in general refers to the evident tendencies or actions of human societies, in which the people who the society perceives to be undesirable or without useful function are excluded i.e. margina.The term defined as marginalization can be in the following ways: Peter Leonard defines - "Marginality as being outside the mainstream of productive activity." Latin observes - "Marginality is so thoroughly demeaning, for economic well-being, for human dignity as well as for physical security marginal people can always be identified by the members of dominant society and will face irrevocable discrimination." The encyclopaedia of public health defines - "Marginalization as to be marginalized is to be placed in the margins as thus excluded from the privilege and power found at the centre." Merriam Webster's online dictionary defines the term marginalization as "To relegate to a un important or powerless position within a society or group". Ghana S Gurung and Michael Kallmair mentions," The concept of marginality is generally, used to analyses socio-economic, political and cultural spheres, where disadvantaged people struggle to gain access to resources and full participation in social life. In other words marginalized people might be socially, economically, politically and legally ignored, excluded or neglected and therefore vulnerable to live hood change

Meaning of Deprived/ Marginalized Groups

The concept of Deprived/ Marginalized Groups is generally used to analyse socioeconomic, political, and cultural spheres, where disadvantaged people struggle to gain access to resources and full participation in social life. In other words, marginalized people might be socially, economically, politically and legally ignored, excluded, or neglected, and, therefore vulnerable. Marginality' is demeaning, for economic well-being, for human dignity, as well as for physical security.

Marginalization/deprived is generally described as the overt actions or tendencies of human societies, where people who they perceive to be undesirable or without useful function are excluded, i.e., marginalized. The people who are Deprived/ Marginalized are outside the existing systems of protection and integration. This limits their opportunities and means for survival.

Nature of Deprived/ Marginalized Groups

Marginalization - is, to place in a position of marginal importance, influence, or power. Deprived/ marginalized is a multidimensional, multi-causal, historical phenomenon. To relegate or confine to a lower or outer limit or edge, as of social standing. There are no general laws to understand and comprehend the complex nature of marginalization. Marginalization can be due to class, in relation to specific social, cultural, economic and political conditions, as well as ideological systems, social awareness, and human action.

Deprived/ Marginalized Groups vary in different settings. The religious, ecological system, patriarchy, political economy of a country, and the overall social system have an impact on the marginalization of specific groups or an individual.

Deprived/ Marginalized also varies from culture to culture. This can be seen in relation to elderly people living in different countries and cultures. The strong and supportive traditional family system in some cultures often provides better respect and care to elders than the public aided system available in others.

Level of awareness among the marginalized groups plays very important role. Organized communities which are aware of their rights, demand more justice than unorganized communities. This also depends upon the support of the political-economic system of the country where they live in. Democratic institutions are favourable for most of the disadvantaged groups.

Deprived/ Marginalized Groups happen simultaneously at the micro and macro levels. Deprived/ Marginalized Groups occurs at different levels, i.e., individual, group, community, and global. Discrimination across different social institutions, such as family, schools and neighbourhood, at work places, or places of worship. Many communities, a result of colonization, experience marginalization such as aboriginals, or women too face discrimination. Globalization too has increased the gap between rich and poor nations. The influx of capitalism, information technology, company outsourcing, job insecurity, and the widening gap between the rich and the poor, impacts the lives of individuals and groups in many capacities.

Process of Marginalization

The process of marginalization can thus be understood as having two aspects. The first aspect of the process of marginalization is that of the inferior location of these groups. They are located on the margins or the periphery. They don't form a part of mainstream society, as the privileged groups do. Such individuals are practically located 'outside' the strata of which they happen to be a part of either by ascription of achievement (Ram 1997). Owing to the 'outside' or the 'peripheral' location they don't enjoy the same benefits as the ones located in the mainstream do. The marginalized are in fact characterized by the least or minimal access to the socio-economic resources available.

The second aspect is the process of social exclusion. In an unequal and hierarchically organized society, not all groups enjoy equal amounts of power and prestige. Some groups or strata enjoy more power and influence at the expense of others. They are placed higher in the hierarchical social order which makes it easier for them to access the desirable goods and position in society. Consequently they are not able to fully participate in economic, social and civic life, and their inadequate access to material and non-material resources, exclude them from enjoying a quality of life and standard of living that is regarded as acceptable in society they live in. This puts them in a position of a major social disadvantage. In this way, the existential location of certain groups is less favorable in the social structural system as compared to other groups. In this sense, they are excluded from the sphere of power, prestige and influence through social, cultural and economic mechanisms.

Types of Deprived/ Marginalized Groups

Marginalization at the individual level results in an individual's exclusion from meaningful participation in society.

Some broad types of Deprived/ Marginalized Groups such as social, economic, and political have been identified.

i) Socially Deprived/ Marginalized Groups

Social marginalisation is a process of social rupture or destruction, in which groups as well as individuals alike become detached from various types of social functions and relations. This generally prevents these people from functioning in the so called normal activities within a society. The individual is forced into a new system of rules while facing social stigma and stereotypes from the dominant group in society. Socially marginalized people are largely deprived of social opportunities. There are those born into marginal groupings e.g., lower castes in India, or members of ethnic groups suffer discrimination. This marginality is typically for life. They lack the required social and cultural capital to participate in mainstream development processes. Their social networks are weak and vulnerable. They are deprived of access to resources, such as, economic, educational, cultural, and other support systems. This creates social isolation and limits their participation in the development process.

ii) Economically Deprived/ Marginalized Groups

Economic marginalization" means being unimportant to the economy. Some individuals or groups can be marginalized from the rest of the economy. The sources and amount of their income varies. Poverty and economic marginalization have both direct and indirect impact on people's health and wellbeing.

iii) Politically Deprived/ Marginalized Groups

Political marginalization does not allow the group to participate democratically in decision making, and, hence, they lose their right to every social, economic, and political benefit. In every society, lack of political empowerment affects large sections of people, including women, ethnic minorities, migrants, and disabled persons, elderly.

Reasons responsible for Deprived/ Marginalized Groups

Some of the important factors that are responsible for marginalization are exclusion, globalization, displacement, and disaster both natural, and manmade.

i) Exclusion: Marginalization is a process that denies opportunities and outcomes to 'those 'living on the margins', while enhancing the opportunities and outcomes for those who are 'at the centre'. Deprived/ Marginalized combines discrimination and social exclusion. It offends human dignity, and it denies human rights. Caste and class prejudice, in many societies across the globe, exclude many groups and communities, and hinder their active participation in economic and social development.

ii) Globalization: Globalization has increased openness which has promoted development at the cost of equity. It is viewed that globalization has enhanced the gap between haves and have-nots and thus boosted marginalization. While it is true that some middle income developing countries, as well as the most populous countries, India and China, are gaining out of globalization, yet the impact is not equally universal.

iii) Displacement: The development programmes implemented by the government and increasing construction of development projects consistently displace a massive number of tribal, poor, and weaker sections. This results in marginalization of already marginalized people.

iv) Disasters- Natural and Unnatural: Disasters are a global phenomena and a serious challenge to development. Vulnerability is linked to broader social issues such as poverty, social exclusion, conflict, education, health, gender issues and marginalization.

Classifications of disasters.

Natural: earthquake, volcanic eruption, hurricane, tornado, ice storm, flood, landslide, wildfire, insect infestation, and disease outbreaks.

Manmade: Can be associated with technological advances, i.e., explosives, unexploded ordinance, toxic spills, emissions of radioisotopes, and transportation accidents. It also includes incidents involving hazardous materials such as carcinogens, mutagens, or heavy metals. Dangers are posed by structural failure of devices and machines or installations, and plants, such as bridges, dams, mines, power plants, pipelines, high rise buildings, vehicles, and trains.

Social: These include incidents primarily involving social unrest, such as hijacking, riots, demonstrations, crowd rushes, and stampedes, terrorist incidents, as well as bombings, shootings, and hostage taking.

Most vulnerable Deprived/ Marginalized Groups

Some of the most vulnerable marginalized groups in almost every society are:

i) Women: Under different economic conditions, and under the influence of specific historical, cultural, legal and religious factors, marginalization of women can be seen from their exclusion from certain jobs and occupations. Women belonging to lower classes, lower castes, illiterate, and the poorest region have been marginalized more than their better off counterparts.

ii) People with Disabilities: People with disabilities have had to battle against centuries of biased assumptions, harmful stereotypes, and irrational fears. The stigmatization of disability resulted in the social and economic marginalization of generations with disabilities, and thus has left people with disabilities in a severe state of impoverishment for centuries.

iii) Elderly: Being past middle age and approaching old age; rather old. S Ageing is an inevitable and inexorable process in life. For most nations, regardless of their geographic location or developmental stage, the 80 year olds, or over-age group is growing faster than any younger segment of the older population. Elderly women form the majority of marginalized groups among them.

iv) Ethnic minority: – a group that has different national or cultural traditions from the majority of the population the term, ethnic minority, refers to marginalised people of the same race or nationality who share a distinctive culture. A minority is a sociological group that does not constitute a politically dominant voting majority of the total population of a given society. It may include any group that is subnormal with respect to a dominant group, in terms of social status, education, employment, wealth, and political power. Every large society contains ethnic minorities. They may be migrant, indigenous or landless nomadic communities, or religious minorities that have a different faith from the majority.

v) Caste Groups: The caste system is a strict hierarchical social system based on underlying notions of purity and pollution. Brahmins are on the top of the hierarchy and Shudras or Dalits orthe Scheduled Castes constitute the bottom of the hierarchy. The marginalization of Dalits influences all spheres of their life, violating basic human rights such as civil, political, social, economic and cultural rights. Literacy rates, purchasing power and poor housing conditions among Dalits are very low. Physical segregation of their settlements is common. However, in recent years due to affirmative action and legal protection, the intensity of caste-based marginalization is reducing.

vi) Tribes: In India, the population of Scheduled Tribes is around 84.3 million and is considered to be socially and economically disadvantaged group. They are mainly landless with little control over resources such as land, forest and water. They constitute agricultural, casual, plantation and industrial labourers. This has resulted in poverty, low levels of education and poor access to health care services. In the Indian context the marginalized are categorized as the scheduled castes, scheduled tribes, denoted tribes, nomadic tribes, and other backward classes.

Problems Related to Education for Deprived/ Marginalized Groups

The challenge of poverty associated with disability: With an estimated 1,027 million people, India is the world's second most populated country. It has 17 percent of the global population and 20 percent of the world's out-of-school children. Despite impressive gains in the last few decades India still has more than 260 million people living in poverty. A large number of children with disabilities live in families with income significantly below the poverty level. While disability causes poverty, it is also possible that in a country like India, poverty causes disability. The combination of poverty and disability results in a condition of "simultaneous deprivation. This is a syndrome that sets up barriers to the participation of persons with disabilities in the normal routines and activities of the community, including regular schooling.

The challenge of modifying deeply held attitudes: Attitudes of the non-disabled are proving to be a major barrier in the social integration of persons with disabilities. "The more severe and visible the deformity is, the greater is the fear of contagion, hence the attitudes of aversion and segregation towards the crippled". Such attitudes reinforced by religious institutions may militate against any attempts to include students with disabilities into regular schools. For example, Hindus believe that disability is a consequence of misdeeds performed in the previous life (often referred to as the doctrine of Karma. Any attempts to improve the life of a person with a disability may be considered a "defiance of the wills of Allah or as interference with a person's karma"

Dissemination and public education: People, including parents and school personnel, are largely unaware of the full intent of the recent legislation passed by Indian Parliament. A large number of school personnel are also not aware of funding available to include students with disabilities in regular schools. There is some evidence that those educators who are knowledgeable about government policies and laws concerning integrated education tend to have positive attitudes toward implementing such programs. There is also evidence when parents are knowledgeable and supportive of integrated education; they tend to have a positive effect on school personnel. Thus, unless people, especially parents of children with disabilities and school personnel, are made knowledgeable about the various provisions enshrined in the Act, the Central and State governments' commitment to providing integrated education will be in vain. Although some attempts are being made to disseminate information about the Persons with Disabilities Act to parents, to government officials and non government organizations, they have been extremely limited in coverage.

The challenge of providing adequate levels of training to key stakeholders: The majority of school personnel in India are not trained to design and implement educational programs for students with disabilities in regular schools. Most teacher training programs in India do not have a unit on Disability Studies. The universities, which do cover some aspects of special education in their teacher training programs, fail to train teachers adequately to work in integrated settings

Inadequate resources: The majority of schools in India are poorly designed and few are equipped to meet the unique needs of students with disabilities. The lack of disability friendly transportation services and accessible buildings are considered by some to be far greater problems than social prejudice and negative attitudes. Both the Central and State governments will have to provide increased resources to this aspect of education to ensure successful implementation of integrated practices in schools.

The marginalized/deprived groups existing in society have historically suffered deprivation in all walks of life in general and in education in particular. Efforts have been made towards economic, social and educational progress of the marginalized people of India. The examination reforms have been suggested right from the time of independence by various committees set up for the purpose There is great diversity in the population and the government of India has passed regulations with respect to inclusion of all irrespective of any kind of disability. There are efforts to provide equal opportunities and inclusion of all in the process of education.

Not only are we aware of the vital role that education plays in counteracting disadvantages over which people have little control, but also its important role in shaping their opportunities for education and wider life chances.

Protecting the rights of, marginalised and vulnerable persons is probably the most overlooked and disregarded area of human rights law. Marginalised groups are generally marginalised by society, making them easy to ignore. Since they only ever represent a small percentage of the population they lack the critical mass that is often needed to successfully assert human rights claims. Furthermore marginalised themselves are often antagonistic towards each other.

Constitution of India gave provisions for free and compulsory education to all children of the nation of the age group 6 to 14 to ensure universalization of primary education. In 2009 the Right of Children for Free and Compulsory Education Act was enacted in India to ensure the same. But this intention is not yet implemented properly even nine years after the Right to Education Act. Even though almost all children were enrolled in the school many of them cannot attend the classes and result in drop out. This increased rate of the drop may be because of their socioeconomic background including ethnicity, caste, economic condition, gender, and religion. Children with special needs also deprived of the education system due to inadequate facilities and specialized training. Many studies found that there exist some exclusionary practices from the part of school authorities in many parts of the country which badly influences the education of children from the marginalized group although the responsible officials in this regard hesitate to admit the fact.

Meaning of Marginalized

Marginalization is a universal tendency related to social stratification. In marginalization opportunities and benefits are denied to the individuals those living on the „margins" while encouraging the opportunities for those who are in the „Centre" of the society (Ramesh, 2013). The lower literacy level of education and the continued discrimination of marginalized in educational institutions pose a major problem.

Marginalization may be of –

? Gender-related

? Culture-related

? Location-related

? Poverty-related or

? Special groups include disabled, gifted children and children living with HIV and Aids, etc. Many communities across the world show prejudice based on caste and class resulting in the exclusion of marginalized people. It may directly affect the attainment of effective endowments in the spheres of education, occupation, and livelihood.

Education of marginalized children:

Present Indian scenario Inequality in educational opportunities has emerged as a major issue in India. It has also become pertinent, as the increasing influence of globalization has jeopardized educational opportunities for the marginalized. Although the provision of basic education in most countries is the responsibility of the State, experience shows that, over the years, the role of the State as the main provider of educational services has reduced owing to privatization and commercialization of education leading to a denial of education for the marginalized groups. Various studies have pointed out that the children from socially and economically deprived communities hardly get any chance to get a minimum level of education and most of them are working children. There is a general agreement about the segment of society that is not attending school and they belong to Scheduled Castes (SC), Scheduled Tribes (ST), minority, urban poor, other backward castes and people living in remote rural areas. It is evidenced that a sizeable part of the child population belonging to socially backward communities living in rural areas is still deprived of basic education. Annual report (2016-17) of National Institution for Minority Educational Institutions states that Scheduled Casts students constitute 13.9% and Scheduled Tribes students 4.9% of the total enrolment. 33.75% of students belong to Other Backward Classes. 4.7% of students belong to Muslim Minority and 1.97% from other Minority Community. According to the response received during the survey, 4.67% of students belong to Muslim Minority and 1.97% is from other Minority Community. Muslim Minority has more male students than females whereas another Minority has more females than males. The development of any society will be evidenced by its literacy rate as well as the education accessibility of its members. The survey results indicate that the national level literacy rate is increasing in a steady manner. In 1951 the literacy rate was 18.32% and in the latest senses report it is 72.98%. But if we are analyzing the progress in categories based on locale, gender social strata, etc. we can observe the drastic disparities and inequalities.

There are a gender and locale difference in educational achievement. Statistical reports support that urban males and females show more educational attainment than rural males and rural females. Educational attainment of females than females, tend to be less than that of male irrespective of locality. The area and gender-based literacy level data from the 2011 census report comprehensively gave the present status of educational accessibility of males and females in different locality separately. When analyzing the literacy rate of the latest census report it is evident that even though the total literacy rate increased over the decade there exist a great disparity between the male and female literacy level. In the majority of the states female literacy level is considerably low than the males. The difference between urban and rural education level is much more terrible. Even after seven decades after independence, there exists inequality in accessing the quality education based on gender as well as locality. In all the states the rural literacy rate is far less than that of the urban population. The literacy rate of the urban population is 84.98 and that of the rural population is 68.91. The gap between rural-urban literacy indicates the inadequate educational facilities of the remote places of India. Besides the differences between the social groups within both rural males and females, there exist inter-gender as well as intragroup differences.

The education level of different social groups is well described in the Government of India, 66th round National Sample Survey Organization. While analyzing the report it is clear that the ST and SC communities are the least educated. Among rural males, only 2.2 percent ST and 2.7 percent SC students reached up to graduation. The status of rural females is worse than this. Only 0.9 percent of ST and 1.1percent SC females are acquiring the graduation level and above. In the higher secondary level also this trend is replicating. The percentage of rural ST males who reached up to higher secondary education is 5.7 and rural ST female is 2.7. It is evident that irrespective of the gender the rural people are less accessible to higher education. In the urban area, the literacy level of marginalized people is better than that of the rural area but lagging behind that of other community.

It is noticed that thelevels of educational accessibility of males of the marginalized section were worse than that of both males and females of the other community and similarly within the same social strata there exist gender wise difference. So while comprehensively analyzing the latest senses report of India it is clear that difference in the level of accessibility of education is greater between the marginalized people and other social groups especially in the higher education sector. The Ministry of Human Resource Development given that dropout rate of primary and upper primary classes were less when compared to the rate of secondary classes. Engagement in economic activities is found to be the reason for the dropout for males from school and females are forced to involve in domestic activities, especially in the rural area.

Inequality in the Quality of Education

Apart from the lack of physical access due to prevailing social biases and economic as well as family reasons, a large number of children drop out because of school-related reasons. Poor teaching standards also seem to be one reason for the drop out of many children and results in inequality inside the classroom. Injustice can possibly be reflected even in the curriculum and content if it does not sensitize children about the practice of injustice in society. Curriculum development initiatives need to consider the development of socially responsible individuals. The crucial need of today is to promote tolerance among students through education so that they can appreciate cultural diversity and protest against all the discriminations. However, the teacher"s role in transacting the content efficiently is another important precondition for achieving quality and also to achieve equality in the learners" achievement level. Availability of qualified and efficient teachers needs immediate attention. Recruitment of an adequate number of teachers to ensure the teacher-pupil ratio of 1:40 (as per the SSA recommendation) in all the elementary schools is another pressing issue in most Indian states, which are experiencing a rapid expansion of elementary schools and increase in enrolment. While the teachers need to understand and appreciate the diverse background of children, it is often experienced that they discourage these children from attending school showing an incidence of relational and cultural injustice.

Although India has already made significant strides in the task of expanding schooling facilities for all children, considering the existing disparities, a multifaceted endeavor is required to make a balance between quality and quantity to ensure its benefits available to all sections of society living in different regions. This should be an integral part of policy interventions for promoting social justice in society. Educational inequality takes different forms in different places which in turn results in the decrease in opportunities for children with low economic background, girls, ethnic, linguistic and socially marginalized group and children with disabilities and specialneeds. So integrating all the children irrespective of the above-mentioned barriers should be the prime objective of the country.

CHAPTER EIGHT

Role of Education, School and Teacher

Role of Education, School and Teacher while dealing with issues of Diversity

Role of Education: Linguistic, Regional and Religious Diversity Education is the common unifying factor that can bring about change in the dividing factors of the country on a large scale. It is being made available everywhere in the country and can thus be utilized to bring together and strengthen the unity of our nation.

Challenges and Role of Education:

Education can help in the following ways:

? **Propagation of national language:** In the event of there being one national language and literature, the people speaking the different languages will have to come in contact with each other through the medium of this national language. Thus the tension existing between them will be sensibly lessened.

? **Encouragement to all major languages:** Along with the development of one common national language and literature, the main regional languages should also be encouraged. No language can be forced upon any region neither can a language be developed by putting stress upon it. The language develops through the medium of usage. The government should encourage all the important regional languages. The government should see to it that Punjabi is developed in Punjab, Bengali in Bengal and so on. In addition to which Hindi should be propagated in all the parts of the country. Building respect for all languages, songs of all languages should be taught, days such as Hindi Divas should be celebrated.

? **Sound Language Policy in Education:** The 3 language formula is given by Kothari Commission which is a modified and revised form of the earlier policy. It equalizes the language burden and also develops the Indian identity in every citizens through the learning of a common language and it has been adopted by all the states.

(a) Mother tongue/Regional language

(b) Official Indian language or associate official Indian languages

(c) Modern Indian language or western language not included in (a) or (b).

? **Reorganisation of the syllabi:** The Curriculum of schools should be organised on the basis of modern India's democratic and secular values.

(a) Primary Level: Importance should be laid on singing national songs telling stories of great men, prayer meetings, folk-songs, patriotic songs and social studies. A sense of national identity should be fostered.

(b) Secondary Level: The priority should be given to ethical and moral education, knowledge of languages and literature, co-curricular activities, as well as social studies. National pride should be encouraged.

(c) University Level: Special emphasis should be placed upon the various social sciences, literatures, languages, culture and art. The concept of unity and nationality should be reinforced.

? **Improvement of textbook:**

(a) Textbooks should be designed to encourage a sense of emotional unity with people living in other parts of the country.

(b) For example: History textbooks have been biased in many forms, hence they should be amended and improved.

(c) A good book which is value based will help to check the growth of communal feelings.

(d) Curriculum and textbooks should be free from religious bias.

? Encouragement of extra-curricular activities: Besides formal education, students should be encouraged to take part in extra-curricular activities. For example,

(a) Celebration of National Days: Students and teachers in co-operation with other members of the community should celebrate such national days as August 15, January 26, October

2.Tribute to various Religious headers on important days. Emphasis on the importance of Democracy/Equality and Brotherhood.

(b) Inter-school competitions, inter-state collaborations that would encourage geographical diversities and respect for each other's standard of living. Emphasis on Essential contribution of different Religions.

(c) Elocution competitions, debates also can be undertaken on themes/topics such as: Nationalism, unity in diversity, every State in this country has its own significant importance, etc. Co-curricular Activities should promote Secularism.

? Development of Inter-Cultural Understanding: Understanding can be promoted by developing a liberal attitude towards other cultures. This is an essential pre-condition for national unity.

(a) For example 1: National Anthem: Students should be taught the meaning of our national anthem and sing it properly in chorus. (b) For example 2: Respect for the National Flag: Students should be taught the importance of the national flag and show due respect to the national flag.

(c) For example 3: Organisation of lectures of National Unity: The gatherings organised for the various purposes and activities of school should be utilized for laying emphasis upon national integration.

(d) General Assembly: Secular Atmosphere - prayers of all religious.

? Integration can be brought about through various subjects: Integration of different subjects can help in creating national and International understanding among the students.

(a) Through Geography, one can highlight the interdependence of various states for their available resources.

(b) Through Trade and Commerce, one can highlight the importance of economic development. If one state lacks behind, then how it affects the whole country. Through this we can also point out at how we all need each other's support in order to bring about development.

(c) Through History, the sense of unity in times like the national struggle for independence can be used as examples for promoting unity. Even the mistakes in history can be used to avoid new ones in the future.

(d) In Literature, the language and folk stories as well as cultures of different regions can be brought to attention and deeply understood, promoting and fostering the feeling of unity.

? National Integration can be brought through inculcation of various Methodologies of Teaching: Various methods of teaching should be followed by the teacher in the classroom. A teacher should always remember that every passing lecture leaves an impact on the students.

(a) Various methodologies should be used in the classroom while teaching, such as: Collaborative learning, Co-operative learning, Jigsaw Method and Role Play

(b) School Project: Project should be initiated in schools for the specific purpose of acquainting students with their country. These projects should increase the knowledge about various parts of the country and thus stimulate love for the country.

? Programmes on National Integration: Movies, documentaries, audio clips, etc. should be shown to the students in the class and a discussion should take place on it. This would help in integrated studies where biased views can be kept aside and students can view the issue from different perspectives.

(a) For example 1: Open Air Theatre: At least four times in a year, plays should be staged in schools for the benefit of students. The themes of these plays should be ancient India, contemporary India, and unity at the time of freedom movement and the promotion of national integration.

(b) For example 2: Exhibition of Films and Organizing Tours: There should be exhibitions of films depicting various aspects of national development and national unity. Organizing tours to places of historical importance will further add to the spirit of nationality.

? Awareness and Abolition of Communal Parties: All the political parties which thrive on religious loyalties should be banned or abolished by the government. Even non-political cultural organizations should always be kept under constant vigil so that they cannot preach communalism.

? Transmission of the Past Heritage: By reminding the people about the glorious moments of history where all Hindus, Muslims and Sikhs combined to safeguard the interest of the country, the feelings of nationalism can be inculcated in the minds of the people.

? Public Opinion: Through mass media efforts should be made for changing the attitude of people towards other communities. People must be made aware of the evils of the communalism.

? Secular Policy: The government should not yield to communal pressures and their negative influence on educational aims and policies. A Secular policy must pervade nationwide in all educational institutions.

? Scientific Temper: Educational system must be reconstructed to emphasize nature of our culture and inculcate secularism and scientific temper among young students.

Role of the Teacher in Curbing Linguism, Regionalism and Religious Diversity

? The curriculum offers appropriate content and activities, but it is the teacher who converts it into productive exercises. Thus creating a suitable climate and motivation to reduce the desired cognitive and affective outcomes.

? The teacher cultivates a broad outlook, a receptive open mind, objectivity and fairness, sensitive responsive to human needs and problems, attitudes of cooperation and tolerance, a feeling of fellowship and compassion, genuine concern for human welfare and progress, global perspective, ability to perceive and think critically as well as judge events and developments all over the world in a balanced way along with the ability to see other's points of view.

? The teacher must be above narrow sectarian views, have a broad outlook and worldmindedness, enable the children to understand man as a 'a human' first, and then an Indianor Russian, be well informed about the ancient, medieval and contemporary world and well versed in human relations. The teacher should also be conscious of the wide variety of human attitudes, motives, life styles, enable every child to understand and internalize all that is good and common in every religion, race, culture and ideology.

? Teach National Integration: i.e. think one self as an Indian first and be aware of other cultures and appreciate it.

The more the people are educated the less they will be inclined towards any rumours or be driven away by the selfish and religious political leaders. Educated Indians will think rationally before taking any actions against any other religion. Education plays an important role, particularly emphasizing on value oriented education, both in schools and colleges. This is important for preventing communal feelings. Education based on traditional cultural ideologies can protect the youth from philosophies and ideologies of hatred. If the citizens are educated they will not be persuaded by the inflammatory speeches given by the political leaders and will think more rationally and logically. Through education we can convince and spread a better message of harmony and tolerance among others. India is unique because of its diversity. Understand, accept, celebrate and appreciate India's diversity. Education should promote national integration through both, co-curricular and curricular activities. Thus, education has a very important role to play in the abolishment of the ideologies that threaten the unity of our nation.

Role of Education, School and Teacher while dealing with issues of Social Inequality:

Social equality is the state of affairs in which all people within a specific society or established group have the same status in certain respects. But, inequality is evident in most aspects of lives which includes racial, ethnic, socio-cultural and economic differences. Along with society, the egos of man create inequality.

Children are not much bothered about such inequalities. But unknowingly, they also become a part of it. They won't purposefully create this but it arises sometimes when not given proper attention.

Types of inequalities in schools:

1. Gender inequality

Not only in schools, but it is also a major problem everywhere. Sometimes, restrictions are imposed on students of a particular gender in schools or they may be discriminated on that basis.

2. Racial inequality

Racial inequalities can occur mainly based on the particular caste, religion or the area a student belongs to. The majority will show a tendency to rule them or to avoid them from mainstream activities. Sometimes, even skin complexion can be the basis of such discrimination. This may very badly affect the confidence and calibre of students.

3. Economic inequality

This is also a worst form of inequality that appears among school children. In a school, students belonging to different financial backgrounds study in the same class. This gap is evident in the cloths the students wear, different accessories and stationeries they use in the class and the cash they bring to the class for their needs. Discrimination based on the financial status can hurt the students and make them feel inferior.

4. Academic inequality

All students don't have the same calibre to learn or to grasp lessons. Their grades also vary. If the teachers show an extra affection towards those who score well, it will badly influence the weak children. The comparison made between the students by teachers and parents can be harmful.

How to solve these inequalities?

- To solve gender inequalities, the teachers and parents involved should work together. The habit of giving priorities for a particular gender should be avoided. Let all students participate in all the activities irrespective of their gender. Discard the activities which don't support mutual participation.
- Racial discrimination should be avoided in schools. All students are equal, no matter what their religion, caste, complexion or locality is. The teacher must not be biased and also, they should take necessary disciplinary actions towards those who pass biased comments and remarks.
- Teach the students the importance of secularism and unity. Make them aware of the feelings of those who are marginalized in the society. Tell them stories and incidents to develop a humanitarian concern in them.
- To solve the economic inequalities, the first thing is to implement uniform for schools and make it compulsory to wear it on all days. The schools should supply the uniform, books, stationeries etc. for them. If possible, the schools should provide lunch too.
- Inform the parents not to give any cash to the students unless the teacher demands.
- Smartcards can be implemented so that the students can make their necessary purchases with that. The students will not have to bring money to the school and spend it unnecessarily because their parents will be aware of every item they purchase with that from school store or canteen.
- To solve the academic inequalities, the teachers must take the upper hand. Always divide the class into groups which includes all levels of students for class activities. Give special attention to those who are weak and bring them up to the level of others.
- Utilize Parent portal for better communication between the teachers and parents. Through Parent Portal, every parent can contact the teachers and get information regarding their child confidentially. They don't have to feel bad about disclosing anything regarding their child to the teacher, so that the teacher can take care of the issue without letting others know about it.

Some of the strategies can be adopted by teachers in order to address issues of inequalities .

- **Rethink ability grouping**

Is ability grouping necessary? Try different ways of organising groups of students in the classroom. Rather than creating separate activities based on a preconceived idea of ability, students could work through tasks with differing levels of challenge. This allows them to think about what they can achieve and does not label anyone incapable.

Try providing more open-ended activities that require the students to problem-solve and draw on a range of skills. For example, see if they can make a tower strong enough to hold a marble with a given set of materials, or invite students to plan a class party that needs invitations, decorations and food.

Allow them to work together – one student may be good at writing while another may be more creative. Students can support each other and surprise themselves and you. Sometimes they will all be given the same task and will produce something different from it (writing stories of different lengths and complexities, for example). The important thing is not to predetermine what students can achieve before they have started.

- **Check your language**

Interrogate the language you use to describe your pupils and the language used by students themselves in the classroom. Nobody is inherently low ability, discourses of "boys will be boys" or "hardworking, helpful girls" limit everyone in the class, as do ideas about "lads" and "bitchy girls" – such double standards need challenging.

Some students still use the term "gay" to describe something negative, which can cause those exploring their own sexuality or who come from queer families to feel unsafe. Using labels such as "naughty" or "silly" to describe pupils, even if not used in front of the students themselves, can quickly stick and alter how students are perceived.

- **Make the curriculum relevant**

Who decides the curriculum? Is it representative of the students in the class, reflecting their experiences, histories and questions? It isn't possible to make the curriculum relevant to all of the students all the time, but consider asking them what they would like to learn about. When I did this with the class of six- and seven-year-olds, we planned out a whole term of activities around the topic of babies, through film, writing and other activities – linking together subjects across the curriculum, and reflecting some of the students' own experiences.

Where it's not possible to alter curriculum material, critical conversations could be started around the points of view represented in lessons from history, science or literature. I've changed my questioning to encourage students to think about whose point of view we are hearing. For example, drawing children's attention to the gender of scientists and suggesting they find out about female scientists; or when we learn about kings and queens, who are we not learning about? – if school resources show only white people in Tudor times, for instance, encourage students to ask questions about why people of colour are not represented.

- **Avoid quick-fix punishments**

Many behaviour management systems in schools are incredibly shaming for students. Having your name written under a sad face, being made to stand up during assembly, or being asked to sit on the floor in another classroom, are publicly humiliating practices that would seem shocking if carried out in an adult place of work.

Such practices are a quick fix in a busy school day but, in the long run, rarely result in behavioural changes from a student. Consider where space could be opened up for conversation rather than punishment. Can the language around bad behaviour be challenged to make room for more compassionate understanding of students who don't so easily conform?

- **Nurture relationships**

Ultimately, all of these methods aim to help prioritise teacher-student relationships and the relationships between students in the classroom. It's these relationships that allow the student to be seen as a person, as opposed to, for instance, a middle-ability child.

When we connect with the students in front of us by respecting them as people, listening to their point of view, acknowledging their difficulties and acting from a place of compassion, we end up being able to critique the assessments the students take, rather than the students themselves. It is from here that we build a classroom, a school and an education system that is more inclusive of everyone.

Maintaining Equity, Equality and Quality

Equality is the provision of equal treatment, access, and opportunity to resources and opportunities (Gunn, 2018). Essentially, everyone gets the same thing, regardless of where they come from or what needs they might have.

Equity is the provision of personalized resources needed for all individuals to reach common goals. In other words, the goals and expectations are the same for all students, but the supports needed to achieve those goals depends on the students' needs (Equity Education, 2019).

Equality focuses on what is fair within the group. Equity highlights what is fair for the individual. In public education, both group and individual needs are important. All students should have equal access to high quality education and once they get it, they should be afforded equitable supports to achieve success.

Standardization

There is another important term in education that is important to consider in the conversation about equality and equity: standardization. Standardization is "the process of making something [or someone] conform to a standard," (Merriam Webster, 2019). The US public education system was built around standardization. Everyone shares the same goals and expectations. Teachers develop their lessons around state adopted standards. Students are required to demonstrate proficiency on standardized tests, normed on the standard scores of kids in other districts and states. Schools are standard-ized.

It is important to note that standardized education can be equal. Every student is expected to meet the same sets of standards, goals, and objectives as their grade-level peers.

Difference between Equity and Equality

The term 'equity' refers to fairness and justice.

The term 'equality' refers to equal opportunity, equal access, equal treatment, equal sharing and division i.e. keeping everyone at the same level.

Equity= Fairness and justice.

It is about taking rationale and logical decision.

Equality= Sameness.

It is mainly about treating everyone equally irrespective of being rationale or not.

Equity focuses on individual needs and requirement. Thus, it is also known as a need- based approach.According to Equality and Human Rights Commission, equality means "ensuring that every individual has an equal opportunity to make the most of their lives and talents."

Equity is about giving people what they need.Equality is not affected by the need of the people or society. Equality gives same thing to all the people, irrespective of their need and demand.

It focuses on giving more to those who need more and less to those who need less.Here, an individual will only get what everyone else gets.

Equity is positive discrimination. It refers to proportional representation (by race, gender, class etc.) to achieve a fair outcome.Equality might give rise to negative discrimination. It does not follow proportionality in representation.

Equity is the means to reach to equality.Equality is the outcome/end result/end goal of the process.

In equitable approach, people are treated fairly but differently.In equality approach, people are treated equally but may be unfairly.

Equity focuses and stresses on social justice, racial justice, social inclusion and social change.Equality does not focus on social and racial justice. Rather, it creates systemic barrier for social inclusion and social security.

Equity is subjective. It differs from situation to situation and from person to person.Equality is measurable. It does not vary and neither matter whoever looks at it.

Equity respects individual differences and diversity.Equality does not give enough value to individual differences and diversity.

Equity justifies things on the basis of quality.Equality justifies things on the basis of quantity.

It identifies the differences and tries to reduce the gap between the groups or race.It is not concerned with the differences or gap between two or more groups or race.

Equity cannot be achieved through equality.Equality can be achieved through equity.

Proper analysis of the existing situation is needed to practice equity approach.No such analysis is needed is needed to practice equality approach.

Equity principle works even if people do not start from the same point.Equality principle can only work if everyone starts from the same place.

Principle of equity is mainly prioritized by the government in its public policy and guiding documents.Principle of equality is usually practiced by most of the private organizations and agencies.

While following the principle of equity, different instruction and action is taken for people of different race, gender or group.While following the principle of equality, there is no differentiated instruction for people of different race, gender or group.

Equity practitioners believe in equitable resource allocation and thus looks everyone differently.Equality practitioners believe in equal resource allocation and thus does not look anyone differently.

Lack of equity i.e. inequity undermines social justice and fairness.Inequality does not always undermine social justice and fairness. However, it might compromise with the actual need of the people/society.

Inequity is worse to equality.Inequality is better than inequity.

Example of gender equity: Giving more nutritious and additional quantity of food to the pregnant and lactating (breastfeeding) women and adolescent girls, based on their dietary requirement.Example of gender equality: Giving equal quantity of food to all the family members including pregnant and lactating (breastfeeding) women, and adolescent girls, irrespective of their nutritional requirement and need.

Example of education equity: Arranging extra classes and giving special attention to the academically weak student in order reduce his/her existing educational achievement gap and improve his/her education and classroom/ school performance. This will ultimately help the individual student to reach his/her fullest potential.Example of education equality: Giving equal attention and equal effort by the teacher to all the student in the classroom/ school OR arranging extra classes for all the student irrespective of their exam grades, marks and classroom/school performance.

Example of resource equity: When distributing a pair of shoes to the football players, giving a right pair of shoes to all the players as per their feet size.Example of resource equality: When distributing a pair of shoes to the football players, giving same size of shoes to all the players without any concern to their feet size.

Example of workplace equity: Difference in salary, benefits and rewards to the employees as per their work performance, expertise and specialty.Example of workplace equality: Same salary, benefits and rewards to all the employees irrespective of the difference in their work performance.

Equality and EquitySource:https://www.mentalfloss.com/article/625404/equity-vs-equality-what-is-the-difference

Role of Education, School and Teacher while dealing with issues of Marginalization

Education of the Marginalized Deprived/ Marginalized Groups in the Indian Context

The Education Commission 1964-66 in its report stressed on the equalization of educational opportunity. One of the most important objectives of education is to equalize opportunity enabling the marginalized, backward or the underprivileged classes to use education for improvement of their conditions. Policies on education 1968, 1986 and 1992 all stressed upon speedy action for the promotion education of the deprived sections of the society.

Mainstreaming the Marginalized. Deprived/ Marginalized Groups

Mainstreaming is the process, to integrate (a student with special needs) into regular school classes. To incorporate into a prevailing group. The prevailing current of thought, influence, or activity. Representing the prevalent attitudes, values, and practices of a society or group.

Policy initiatives for retracing the Universalisation of Elementary Education (UEE)

Indian constitution has given due emphasis for national integration and hence a national system of education. The directive principles of State Policy envisage that the state shall provide free and compulsory education for children up to fourteen years of age. Later this has been made a fundamental right by amending the Constitution. Constitution of India, through Article 46 entrust the State to promote economic and educational interests of the marginalized and weaker sections of its citizens, especially Scheduled Tribes and Scheduled Castes and also to protect them from social exploitation and all form of social injustice. There are many other articles which help in the implementation of Article 46 like Articles 330, 332, 335, 338 to 342. Fifth and Sixth Schedules of the Indian Constitution also discussing the same objectives. The National Policy on Education (1986) and its POA, 1992 advocate for the provision of essential facilities for attaining universal access to education of comparable quality. Also the Central Advisory Board on Education (CABE), I992 recommended for the adoption of a holistic approach to address the educational needs of children who has to work for their livelihood, girls, disadvantaged and marginalized groups and considering issues of quality, process, and content more efficiently. Drawing experiences from all the earlier programs and projects, District Primary Education Programme (DPEP) was introduced in selected districts in a joint partnership of government and international organizations in 1994. This project was later merged into another national program,

Sarva Shiksha Abhiyan (SSA), which is followed by Rashtriya Madhyamik Siksha Abhiyan (RMSA). These programs have stressed the reduction of the social and gender gap in elementary education. Regional disparities also exist in terms of making provision for educational opportunities. The government should take a second look at the effectiveness of Education Policies and develop and implement major programs for strengthening the accessibility of quality education withoutany objections. A reallocation of government resources for better education and vocational training is the need of the present time. It is a fact that for millions of economically and socially backward students living in rural areas, government loan schemes are still a dream. The solution for this dilemma is the development of a uniform, affordable and quality public education system. If the public education system of a country is strong enough, the chance for discrimination will decrease to a great extent. Mainstreaming the Marginalized Mainstreaming is the process of incorporating individuals with special and specific needs and into the main educational stream to enjoy regular school classes and thus to incorporate them into the prevailing social activities and thoughts. Various initiatives and efforts have been made to realize the concept of education for all however, the rate of wastage and stagnation in the Indian education system is still is in a critical range. Multiple causes are there including social, economic, ethnic and also faulty educational systems which hindering the children from lower social strata from accessing and sustaining the education.

The disturbing trend of dropouts after initial enrolment forces one to ponder over qualitative aspects of schooling and the real classroom experiences of the children coming from the marginalized sections of society. In other words, one needs to adopt a framework of social justice which Looks beyond the aggregate concerns and towards the factors of social justice, identity issues and pedagogical corlcerns. The learning environment provided to these children is often characterized by poor infrastructure, lack of basic amenities and less than adequate number of teachers. Data on the state of schools in rural areas, backward villages and adivasi areas confirm this observation. Such schools account for a poor learning environment and have a negative impact on the motivational and aspirational levels of the students as well as the parents. Centralized curriculum represents yet another issue. Krishna Kumar (1989) 5 maintains that centralized curriculum reflects the culture and social existence of the mainstream groups. It fails to draw upon the factors, objects, experiences and issues, which the children of marginalized minorities live with. It, therefore, doesn't talk about the socio-cultural lives of these children On the one hand such a curriculum fails to relate to the knowledge base of the students who find it irrelevant and meaningless, and on the other it also affects their self-identity and feeling of self-worth in a negative way. This leads to a conflict in the young minds, and an overall sense of disillusionment which is often large enough to force children to drop out of the formal scheme of education. The curriculum is further characterized by the creation, and reinforcement of stereotypes of the marginalized sections that are often presented as negative. Hence, as Krishna Kumar (1989) suggests, the SCs and STs are often depicted as 'culturally backward'. Nambissan (2000) mentions that these communities are largely portrayed in subservient roles in accordance with what is perceived as their traditionally low position in the social hierarchy. This further feeds the discriminatory practices and adverse peer and teacher attitude in the schools, which contributes to a feeling of demotivation and discouragement In the students, besides damaging their self-identity. Similar issues emerge due to gender sterq6types in the formal curriculum. Textbooks have been criticized for depict' g women in traditional roles and stereotypical fashion, which leads to a set i" ing of negative' role models for the girl child. This also, strengthens the patriarchal state of mind and encourages the girl child to conform to the standards without questioning them or looking for better alternatives. It is in fact full of gender stereotypes and fails to construct new ways of viewing and establishing social relations between menand women. The effect of the biased textbooks further shows up in discriminatory practices adopted by teachers and peers. SCs and STs are often ridiculed, avoided and discriminated against due to the traditional low socioeconomic status. overt act of discrimination such as segregation in seating arrangements, refusal to let them use the common pitcher for drinking water, or to touch them and their notebooks and so on are not unheard of . Low expectations and lack of encouragement, also, show up in the poor performance of SC, ST and girl children. Furthermore, the formal curriculum is based on a model of direct instruction by the teacher, who holds authority and power. He is often supposed to discipline children's body and minds by encouraging a culture of rote learning. Such a classroom culture is often based on direct instruction from the teacher, where students are expected to take down notes, memorize and reproduce it in the exams without questioning either the process or the content. The teacher therefore, fails to provide any special assistance or creative support to these children, who often are first generation learners. With a knowledge base that is completely alien and a classroom environment that remains non-supportive, these children lose motivation to do well and complete schoolingFurthermore, schools often fail to use their mdther tongue as the medium of instruction. A number of policy documents have stressed on the pedagogical and cultural importance of the use of the mother tongue in schools, especially at the primary levels , but adivasis languages and local dialects find no place in the classroom. In fact they are discouraged and even ridiculed. This not only further alienates the child from the classroom, but also raises serious problems in comprehension and understanding, evident in the large number of failures and poor performance. The exclusion of the child's language and culture'from the medium and the content of school knowledge as well as the messages of inferiority and confirmation that are conveyed to the children are likely to affect the motivation and aspiration in the negative way.

This account for the loss of interest and lack of effort to continue and gets reflected in the poor retention rates. Thus, what is required is a change in the formal curriculum to be able to accommodate the wider social reality and serious effort in order to give a place of rightful respect and dignity to these sections of society and their socio-cultural and economic environment. The formal curriculum should be able to voice the experiential reality of the Dalits, adivasis and the girl children to enable them to relate and derive meaning and relevance out of it. From the point of view of the girl child, it makes sense to give place in the curriculum to, an examination of women's subordination throughout history, women's contribution and participation in history-making, the value of work commonly performed by women - such as domestic work, the importance of women in the processes of decision-making, participation and organisation, and the incorporation of women's way of knowing and focus on women's experiences. This in effect means giving a more critical approach to the curriculum. Change in curriculum would, however, remain useless and ineffective unless a corresponding change in the pedagogical culture and teacher attitude is initiated which is more sensitive to, and shows a greater understanding of the social and pedagogical issues of the marginalized.

Pedagogical Consideration of Marginalised Group of Students

The basic egalitarian premise in this matter has been that a uniform common curriculum, if not also a common school, leads to equality or lack of ciisprivliege in education. The light that psychology and educational theory throws on this matter tends to suggest, however, some modifications. First, human capacities and capabilities are not uniformly distributed. Thus with in a common school or a common curriculum, different pupils have to be helped to proceed at their own pace. To the extent that schools can provide for this through their own media or methods, etc., it might be desirable to present even the same curriculum through different media and methods. A more extreme view, which would have some justification, would be that a specialized curriculum, particularly after a common period of elementary or secondary schooling, would be farier to individuals with different manual, aesthetic, linguistic , numerical or social potentials. Too rigid an insistence on uniform schooling can, in fact handicap children from less privileged backgrounds, while if it is too differentiated it could perpetuate these distinctions. The development of multipurpose, multilateral or multifaceted secondary educational higher education for different fields might be seen as a measure of equity, minimizing disprevilege. On the.other hand, too specific a secondary or elementary education, without adequate emphases on linguistic and numerical skills, might provide a dead-end education which would handicap the individuals undergoing it. If the allocation of individuals to those specific courses appears related to or based on the caste or class origin of the pupils, the school would be perpetuating social inequalities already in existence, or even accentuating them" (Shukla 2002 : 320-21).

Efforts have been made to reach education to all. However, there is wastage and stagnation in education. There are economic, social and educational causes that hinder the education of children coming from lower strata of society.

- Incentives to families to send their children regularly to schools till they reach the age of 14.
- Pre-metric scholarships for all children regardless of incomes.
- Constant micro planning and verification to ensure enrolment, retention and successful completion of courses.
- Remedial measures to better their chances for further education and employment.

- Recruitment of teachers from scheduled castes.
- Provision of hostel facilities.
- Location of school buildings, balwadis, and adult education centres to facilitate participation especially in rural areas, hill and desert districts or remote and inaccessible areas.
- Priority given to opening schools in tribal areas with help of tribal welfare schemes.
- Developing curricula and instructional materials in tribal languages with facility to switch to regional language.
- Also
- The curricula in the states to depict rich cultural identity of the tribal people.
- Teacher training to tribal youth with assured employment.

Residential schools including ashram schools, anganwadis, non formal and adult education centres to open on priority basis.

Incentive schemes, scholarships for higher education with emphasis on technical, professional and Para-professional courses.

Remedial programmes to help overcome psycho-social impediments.

For the mainstreaming of the marginalized children the following suggestions would be beneficial;

? The effective implementation of the Right to Education Act should be monitored by the government to ensure not simply enrolment of students, but on the retention of every student in school.

? The government should take initiatives to check the dropout rate by monitoring children at risk of dropping out, and develop appropriate social mapping strategies has to develop by relevant authorities among marginalized and minority communities to ensure the retention.

? Any kind of discrimination should be stopped from all the educational systems including from the part of the policymakers, officials, teachers, and fellow students. The government should strictly monitor such practices in the educational institutions from primary level to higher education. National Commission for Protection of Child Rights can do much in this regard by making appropriate guidelines to address discrimination and other abuses of children and set out appropriate disciplinary measures. Penalty for such malpractices also should be strengthening.

? Better incentives to the families to send their children to school regularly till they complete their high school education.

? More teachers should be recruited from various marginalized groups to motivate more students to come to higher education fields

? Better hostel facilities for the students who need it to complete their course

? More educational institutes in rural and remote areas

? Proper attention for the tribal education by giving due respect to their cultural uniqueness and ethnicity ? Designing and implementation of instructional materials and curricula in tribal language with facilities to switch to regional language

? Human Resource Development Ministry can develop manuals for teachers and instructors to foster social inclusion and equity. Encouragement of children from marginalized groups in different school activities and responsibilities would positively influence their development. The collaboration of children of different social strata also should be ensured.

The government can give instruction regarding this. Along with proper service conditions, training and qualifications of teachers are a matter of concern. Quality of education is affected because of teaching-learning materials. Many of the teachers and students hardly get textbooks and materials of good quality causing learning difficulties for the poor children, as they have practically no access to any material other than textbooks. While improving quality, it is necessary to provide essential physical and academic facilities in the school.

Government Schemes. Projects /Programmes for dealing with Issues of Diversity, Inequality anf Marginalization

Education is very important for economic, political, and social transformation. In the twenty-first century, a population that is well-educated and equipped with relevant skills, attitudes, and knowledge is needed for the overall development of society. Education plays a key role in creating a just and equitable society.

India's population is around 1.32 billion. The education system in this country has gone through a lot of changes over the years as per the growing needs and demands. The standard of education in India has been getting better and many children are securing higher marks through quality education. This is because the government is trying to encourage children with the help of various schemes that provide better facilities. They have implemented many changes that are aimed at improving the standard and style of training and teaching. Many state governments have taken steps to send a few teachers to foreign educational institutions to update their skills and knowledge and to improve their teaching quality.

1. Sarva Shiksha Abhiyan (SSA)

This program was introduced in 2001 and is one of the biggest projects in India. The Sarva Shiksha Abhiyan (SSA) is a flagship program for the children to get Universal Elementary Education (UEE). This program covers the entire country and works in partnership with local and state governments. SSA is mainly useful for children between the ages of 6 to 14. The program aims to universalise education and improves its quality by time-bound implementation strategy and context-specific planning. It includes children from all social classes.

2. National Program for Education of Girls at Elementary Education (NPEGEL)

The NPEGEL program has been initiated by the Government of India to reach girls, especially the girls that are not enrolled in a school. The program was started in July 2003 and this program is a significant component of the SSA. The program provides extra support for improving the education of girls. Some objectives that come under this scheme are the development of learning materials that are gender-sensitive, gender-sensitisation of teachers, provisions like stationary, uniforms, and workbooks. The main focus of this program is to break gender stereotypes and to make sure girls get a good education at the elementary level.

3. Midday Meal Scheme

Otherwise known as the National Programme of Nutritional Support to Primary Education, this plan was launched in 1995 to provide mid-day meals to children studying in primary class. The main objective of creating this scheme was to eliminate classroom hunger of children and to increase attendance and enrolment of children at schools. This scheme also aims to improve the interaction between children of all castes and religions. It also addresses the issue of inadequate and improper nutrition among children. Women are also socially empowered since the scheme creates employment opportunities. Thus, this scheme can help in developing children emotionally and socially.

4. Right to Education (RTE) Act

This was another amazing step taken by the government. The Right to Education (RTE) Act was enacted in 2009, and this Act made education for every child between 6 and 14 years a fundamental right. It also set the basic norms that must be followed by every elementary school in the country. Thus, children got the right to receive free elementary education. This means that no child has to pay any kind of charges or fee to complete education up to elementary level. The RTE act also aims at the development of a curriculum that makes sure the child receives the benefit of all-round development, building their knowledge, talent, and potential. The Right to Education Act has made it compulsory to reserve 25 per cent in private schools for children from economically weaker families.

5. Beti Bachao, Beti Padhao

This scheme initiated in 2015 is one of the most famous central government schemes for girl education. The main aim of this government scheme was initially to protect girl children from female foeticide and infanticide and later, provide assistance for their education. Other objectives of the plan include stopping the practice of gender-determination tests and discrimination against girl children. The Beti Bachao, Beti Padhao scheme ensures the protection of girls and their survival and makes sure that girls participate in educational activities alongside boys. This scheme thus spreads the awareness that girl children are not a burden.

6. Kasturba Gandhi Balika Vidyalaya

Launched in 2004, the KGBV scheme aims at setting up residential schools for girls belonging to minority communities at the upper primary level. This scheme is mainly implemented in the parts of the country where girls aren't enrolled in school. This scheme provides reservation of 25% to girls from families below the poverty line and the rest 75% to the girls belonging to ST, SC, OBC, and other minority communities. The main idea behind this scheme is that by setting up residential schools, girls from disadvantaged groups of the society can access quality education.

7. Scheme for Infrastructure Development in Minority Institutes (IDMI)

To improve the quality of education, the scheme has been started to improve infrastructure in unaided/aided minority schools. The salient features of this scheme include expanding facilities that will help the education of children from minority communities. The entire country comes under this scheme, but preference is given to places that have a minority population above 20 per cent. The scheme also encourages educational facilities for children with special needs, girls, and others who are mostly held back in society.

8.The Rashtriya Madhyamik Shiksha Abhiyan: A Centrally sponsored scheme with a funding pattern of 75:25 between Centre and States (90:10 for Special Category and North Eastern States), was launched in 2009–10. The major objectives of theRMSA are to (i) raise the minimum level of education to class X and universalise access to secondary education; (ii) ensure good-quality secondary education with focus on Science, Mathematics and English; and (iii) reduce the gender, social and regional gaps in enrolments, dropouts and improving retention. The interventions supported under RMSA included (i) upgrading of upper primary schools to secondary schools; (ii) strengthening of existing secondary schools; (iii) providing additional classrooms, science laboratories, libraries, computer rooms, art, craft and culture rooms, toilet blocks and water facilities in schools; (iv) providing in-service training of teachers; and (v) providing for major repairs of school buildings and residential quarters for teachers. Despite being launched in the third year of Plan, there was good progress under the RMSA during the Eleventh Plan . Against a target of enrolling an additional 3.2 million students, 2.4 million additional students were enrolled in secondary schools during the Eleventh Plan period.

9.Scheme for Setting up of 6000 Model Schools at Block Level: The Scheme envisages providing quality education to talented rural children through setting up 6000 model schools as benchmark of excellence at block level at the rate of oneschool per block. The scheme was launched in 2008-09 and is being implemented from 2009-10. The objectives are:

? To have at least one good quality senior secondary school in every block.

? To have a pace setting role.

? To try out innovative curriculum and pedagogy

? To be a model in infrastructure, curriculum, evaluation and school governance. The scheme has two modes of implementation, viz., (i) 3500 model schools are to be set up in educationally backward blocks (EBBs) under State/ UT Governments; and (ii) the remaining 2500 schools are to be set up under Public-Private Partnership (PPP) mode in the blocks which are not educationally backward. Presently, only the component for setting up of 3500 model schools in EBBS under State/UT Governments is operational. The component for setting up of 2500 model schools under PPP mode will be operational in 12th Five Year Plan

10.Scheme of Vocationalisation of Secondary Education at +2 level: Initiated in 1988, this centrally sponsored scheme of Vocationalisation of Secondary Education provides for diversification of educational opportunities so as to enhance individual employability, reduce the mismatch between demand and supply of skilled manpower and provides an alternative for those pursuing higher education10 . Hence, it is important and would be implemented from class IX onwards, unlike the present provision for its implementation from class XI, and would be subsumed under RMSA. Vocational Education courses will be based on national occupation standard brought out by the Sector kill Councils (SSCs) that determine the minimum levels of competencies for various vocations. Academic qualifications would be assessed and certified by educational bodies and vocational skills would be assessed and certified by respective SSCs.

11.Scheme of ICT @ School: The Information and Communication Technology in School Scheme was launched in December 2004 to provide opportunities to secondary stage students to mainly build their capacity of ICT skills and make them learn through computer aided learning process. The Scheme provides support to States/Union Territories to establish enabling ICT infrastructure in Government and Government aided secondary and higher secondary schools. It also aims to set up Smart schools in KVs and Navodaya Vidyalayas which are pace setting institutions of the Government of India to act as "Technology Demonstrators" and to lead in propagating ICT skills among students of neighbourhood schools

12.Inclusive Education for Disabled at Secondary stage: The Scheme of Inclusive Education for Disabled at Secondary Stage (IEDSS) has been launched from the year 2009-10. This Scheme replaces the earlier scheme of Integrated Education for Disabled Children (IEDC) and would provide assistance for the inclusive education of the disabled children in classes IX-XII. The aim of the Centrally Sponsored Scheme of IEDSS is to enable all students with disabilities, after completing eight years of elementary schooling, to pursue further four years of secondary schooling (classes IX to XII) in an inclusive and enabling environment

13.Adult Education and Skill Development Schemes Adult Education aims at extending educational options to those adults, who have lost the opportunity and have crossed the age of formal education, but now feel a need for learning of any type, including, basis education (literacy), skill development (Vocational Education) etc. In order to promote adult education and skill development through the voluntary sector, support to Voluntary Agencies (Vas) was so far being extended through two schemes, namely, (i) Assistance to Voluntary Agencies in the field of Adult Education and (ii) Jan Shikshan Sansthans. With effect from 1 April 2009 both these schemes have been merged and a modified scheme, named as "Scheme of Support to Voluntary Agencies for Adult Education and Skill Development" has been put up in place. The Scheme encompasses three components, namely, State Resource Centres, Jan Shikshan Sansthans and Assistance to Voluntary Agencies1

14. Scheme for Providing Quality Education for Madrsas(SPQEM) SPQEM seeks to bring about qualitative improvement in madrsas to enable Muslim children attain standards of the national education system in formal education subjects. The salient features of SPQEM scheme are: i) To strengthen capacities in Madrsas for teaching of the formal curriculum subjects like Science, Mathematics, Language, Social Studies etc through enhanced payment of teacher honorarium. ii) Training of such teachers every two years in new pedagogical practices. iii) The unique feature of this modified scheme is that it encourages linkage of madarsas with National Institute for Open Schooling (NIOS), as accredited centres for providing formal education, which will enable children studying in such madarsas to get certification for class 5,8,10 and 12. This will enable themto transit to higher studies and also ensure that quality standards akin to the national education system. Registration & examination fees to the NIOS will be covered under this scheme as also the teaching learning materials to be used. iv) The NIOS linkage will be extended under this scheme for Vocational Education at the secondary and higher secondary stage of madarsas.

15.Eklavya Model Residential Schools (EMRSs): These schools are funded by the Government for the welfare of Scheduled Tribes. Proposals for setting of EMRS are received from the State Government. The Ministry of Tribal Affairs administers special area programme of grant under Art 275 (1) of the Constitution of India. Under this programme State wise allocation to 26 States including 9 Left Wing Extremism (LWE) States is made on the basis of percentage of Scheduled Tribes population in the State with reference to total ST population in the Country. A part of the grant can be used for setting up of Eklavya Model Residential Schools (EMRS). Priority for the development schemes including setting up of EMRS is fixed and executed by the State Government within the allocation depending on the felt need of the local area and its people in accordance with the guidelines issued by the Ministry in June 2010

16.Pre-matric Scholarship Scheme: Pre-matric is the Scholarship for students from Minorities Communities. The Scholarship at Pre-matric level will encourage parents from minority communities to send their school going children to school, lighten their financial burden on school education and sustain their efforts to support their children to complete school education. The scheme will form the foundation for their educational attainment and provide a level playing field in the competitive employment arena. Empowerment through education, which is one of the objectives of this scheme, has the potential to lead to upliftment of the socio economic conditions of the minority communities.

CHAPTER NINE

Constitutional Provisons, Policies and Acts in Education

Constitutional Provisions for Education in India

Some of the major constitutional provisions on education in India are as follows:

There are some changes regarding the 42nd Amendment to the Constitution. During 1976 our constitution was amended in many of its fundamental provisions. Under the Constitution of India, the Central Government has been specifically vested with several educational responsibilities.

Below are given constitutional provisions on Education:

1. Free and Compulsory Education:

The Constitution makes the following provisions under Article 45 of the Directive Principles of State Policy that, "The state shall endeavour to provide within a period of ten years from the commencement of this Constitution, for free and compulsory Education for all children until they complete the age of fourteen years."

The expression 'State' which occurs in this Article is defined in Article 12 to include "The Government and Parliament of India and the Government and the Legislature of each of the States and all local or other authorities within the territory of India or under the control of the Government of India." It is clearly directed in Article 45 of the Constitution that the provision of Universal, Free and Compulsory Education becomes the joint responsibility of the Centre and the States.

In the Constitution it was laid down that within 10 years, i.e., by 1960 universal compulsory education must be provided for all children up to the age of 14, But unfortunately, this directive could not be fulfilled. Vigorous efforts are needed to achieve the target of 100 percent primary education. The Central Government needs to make adequate financial provisions for the purpose. At the present rate of progress it may, however, be expected that this directive may be fulfilled by the end of this century.

2. Education of Minorities:

Article 30 of the Indian Constitution relates to certain cultural and educational rights to establish and administer educational institutions.

It lays down:

(i) All minorities whether based on religion or language, shall have the right to establish and administer educational institutions of their choice.

(ii) The state shall not, in granting aid to educational institutions, discriminate against any educational institution on the ground that it is under the management of a minority, whether based on religion or language.

3. Language Safeguards:

Article 29(1) states "Any section of the citizen, residing in the territory of India or any part there of having a distinct language, script or culture of its own, hall have the right to conserve the same." Article 350 B provides for the appointment of special officer for linguistic minorities to investigate into all matters relating to safeguards provided for linguistic minorities under the Constitution.

4. Education for Weaker Sections:

Article 15, 17, 46 safeguard the educational interests of the weaker sections of the Indian Community, that is, socially and educationally backward classes of citizens and scheduled castes and scheduled tribes. Article 15 states, "Nothing in this article or in clause (2) of Article 29 shall prevent the state from making any special provision for the advancement of any socially and educationally backward classes of citizens or for the scheduled castes and the scheduled tribes."

Under Article 46 of the Constitution, the federal government is responsible for the economic and educational development of the Scheduled Castes and Scheduled Tribes

It states. "The state shall promote with special care the educational and economic interests of the weaker sections of the people and in particular, of the Scheduled castes and Scheduled Tribes and shall protect them from social injustice and all forms of exploitation." It is one of the Directive Principles of State Policy.

5. Secular Education:

India is a secular country. It is a nation where spirituality based on religion, had always been given a high esteem. Under the Constitution, minorities, whether based on religion or language, are given full rights to establish educational institutions of their choice. Referring to the constitutional provisions that religious instructions given in institutions under any endowment or Trust, should not be interfered with even if such institutions are helped the State.

Article 25 (1) of the Constitution guarantees all the citizens the right to have freedom of conscience and the right to profess, practice and propagate religion.

Article 28 (1) states, "No religious instruction shall be provided in any educational institution if wholly maintained out of state fund."

Article 28 (2) states, "Nothing in clause (1) shall apply to an educational institution which is administered by the State but has been established under any endowment or Trust which requires that religious instruction shall be imparted to such institution."

Article 28 (3) states, "No person attending any educational institution by the state or receiving aid out of state funds, shall be required to take part in any religious instruction that may be imported in such institutions or to attend any religious worship that may be conducted in such institution or in any premises attached thereto unless such person or, if such person a minor, his guardian has given his consent thereto."

Article 30 states, "The state shall not, in granting aid to educational institution maintained by the State or receiving aid out of State funds, on grounds only of religion, race, caste, language or any of them."

6. Equality of Opportunity in Educational Institutions:

Article 29(1) states "No citizen shall be denied admission into any educational institution maintained by the State or receiving aid out of State funds, on grounds only of religion, race, caste, language or any of them."

The Fundamental Rights of the Indian Constitution has also adopted the fourfold ideal of justice, Liberty, Equality and Fraternity. Our Constitution laid down that in the eyes of law, everyone should have an equal status, to no one the justice be denied, everyone should have liberty of thought, expression.

The fundamental right of equality clearly signifies that in the eyes of law no distinction can be made on the basis of any position, caste, class or creed. Side by side the right of equality of opportunities to all is also provided. The equality of opportunity is meaningless, unless there are equal opportunities for one's education.

The well-known Kothari Commission, 1964-66 recommended that Central Government should undertake the responsibility in education for the equalization of educational opportunities with special reference to the reduction of inter-state differences and the advancement of the weaker section of the community.

7. Instruction in Mother -Tongue:

There is diversity of languages in our country. After the dawn of Independence, Mother- Tongues have received special emphasis as medium of instruction and subjects of study. In the Constitution of India, it has been laid down that the study of one's own language is a fundamental right of the citizens.

Article 26 (1) states, "Any section of the citizens, residing in the territory of India or any part there of, having a distinct language, script or culture of its own, shall have the right to converse the same."

Article 350 A directs, "It shall he endeavour of every state and every local authority to provide adequate facilities for instruction in the mother-tongue at the primary stage of education to children belonging to linguistic minority groups."

Secondary Education Commission, 1952-53 recommended that the mother tongue or the regional language should generally be the medium of instruction throughout secondary school stage subject to the provision that for linguistic minorities, special facilities should be made available. Kothori Commission, 1964-66 has also said that at college and university stage, mother-tongue should be the medium. The medium of instruction at school level is already mother-tongue. This is not a new proposal.

8. Promotion of Hindi:

The Indian Constitution makes provision for the development and promotion of Hindi as national language. Article 351 enjoins the Union, the duty to promote the spread of the Hindi language.

Hindi accepted as the Official Language of India as laid down by the Constitution in following words:

"It shall be the duty of the Union to promote the spread of the Hindi language, to develop it so that it may serve as a medium of expression of all the elements of the composite culture of India." In practice, Hindi is already largely in use as a link language for the country. The educational system should contribute to the acceleration of this process in order to facilitate the movement of student and teacher and to strengthen national Unity.

9. Higher Education and Research:

Parliament has the exclusive rights to enact legislation in respect of institutions and Union Agencies mentioned in entries 63, 64, 65, and 66 of List. The entries which give authority to the Government of India in education are mentioned below:

Entry 63 of the Union List:

The institutions known at the commencement of this Constitution as the Banaras Hindu University, the Aligarh Muslim and the Delhi University, and any other institution declared by Parliament by law to be an Institution of National importance.

Entry 66 of the Union List:

Co-ordination and determination of standards in institution for higher education or research and scientific and technical institutions.

10. Women's Education:

One of the unique features of Modem Indian Education is the tremendous advancement of Women's Education. Education of the girls is considered to be more important than that of the boys.

The Constitution makes the following provisions under different articles:

Article 15(1) provides that the State shall not discriminate any citizen on groups only of sex.

Article 15 (3) reads: "Nothing in this article shall prevent the State from making any special provision for women and children."

The well-known National Policy on Education was concerned about the status and education of women in the country. It envisages that education would be used as a strategy for achieving a basic change in the status of women. It opined that the national system of education must play a positive role in this direction.

The Policy states, "Education will be used as an agent of basic change in the status of women. In order to neutralize the accumulated distortions of the past, there will be a well conceived edge in favour of women."

11. Education in the Union Territories:

Article 239 of the Constitution states, "Save as otherwise provided by Parliament by Law, every Union Territory shall be administrator by the president acting to such extent as he thinks fit through an administrator to be appointed by him with such designation as he may specify."

12. Educational and cultural relations with foreign countries:

Entry 13 of the Union List reads. Participation in international conferences, associations and other bodies and implementing decisions made there at.

Right of free and compulsory education

Article-45

The state shall endeavour to provide within the period of 10 years from the commencement of this constitution, for free and compulsory education for all children until they complete the age of 14 years." – Article 45, Directive Principles of State Policy.

Article 45 of the constitution provides the provision for free and compulsory education.

India has set lofty educational development goals since its independence.

According to the Kothari Commission, ensuring free and universal education for all children is a top educational priority, not only for social justice and democracy but also for improving average worker competence and increasing national productivity.

Universalization has the following problems:

Lack of financial resources

Very small villages

Lack of suitable buildings

The poverty of Parents and their non-co-operation

Providing suitable staff and facilities

Indifference to primary education and dropout of students without completing primary education

Right to education

Constitutional Acts related to Education

Right to Education Act 2009 is a constitutional act related to education in the Indian Constitution. This act has come into force on April 1, 2010. This act gives the Right to Education the same legal status as the right to life.

Section 21(A) –

The state shall provide free and compulsory education to all children aged 6 to 14 years in the manner determined by law (86 amendment, Act 2002).

The Constitution (Eighty-sixth Amendment) Act, 2002 inserted Article 21-A into the Indian Constitution, declaring right to education a Fundamental

Amendment 93 (Primary Education a Fundamental Right) –

Primary education is now a 'Fundamental Right' under the 93rd amendment to the constitution. It is now a legal right.

Education for women

One of the prominent elements of contemporary Indian education and its policies is the promotion of women's education.

The education of girls is regarded as equally vital as that of boys.

The following provisions are made in several articles of the Constitution:

Article 15 This article prohibits discrimination against any citizen on the basis of gender, religion, race, or place of birth.

Article 15 (3) of the constitution empowers the state to create specific provisions for women, including education.

Article 15(1) According to this article, the state shall not discriminate against any citizen on the basis of gender, religion, race, or place of birth.

The 1986 National Policy on Education was especially concerned with the status and education of women in the country.

According to the Education Policy of 1986, "education would be employed as an agent of fundamental change in the status of women in the society."

Constitutional Provisions for education of SC and ST in India

The Indian constitution requires the government to promote the educational interests of the socially, culturally, and economically disadvantaged sections of society.

There are many provisions made in our constitutions for the upliftment of weaker sections of our society like, Article 14, 15, 46, 46, 338, 339 and 340.

Out of many such articles, article 15 and 46 of the constitution give provisions related to the education of SC and ST (weaker sections) in India

Article 46 states that "The state shall promote with special care the educational and economic interests of the weaker sections of the society, particularly the Scheduled Castes and Scheduled Tribes, and shall protect them from social injustice and all types of exploitation".

It is one of the directive principles of state policy.

Education of minorities, protection of interests of minorities

These constitutional provisions (Article 29 and 30) ensure that minorities' special interests are protected. Minorities are classified according to their religion, linguistic script, or culture.

Article 29- This article is related to the education, rights and interests of minorities. This means that the constitution provides certain safeguards for the cultural and educational interests of minorities. It states that

29(1)- Any section of the citizen, residing in the territory of India or any part there of having a distinct language, script or culture of its own, hall have the right to conserve the same.

29(2)- No citizen shall be denied admission into any educational institution maintained by the state or receiving aid out of state funds on grounds only of religion, race, caste, language or any of them.

Right of minorities to establish and administer educational institutions

Minorities are granted the ability to establish and administer their own educational institutions by the Constitution of India. Article 30 is sometimes known as the "Charter of Education Rights." This article states that

"All minorities whether based on religion or language shall have right to establish and administer educational institutions of their choice".

"The states shall not discriminate against any educational institution in respect of granting aid, on the ground that it is under the management of a minority whether based on religion or language"

Instruction in mother-tongue at primary stage

Our country is multilingual. The Indian Constitution establishes that the study of one's own language is a fundamental right of citizens.

The Secondary Education Commission of 1952–53 proposed that the mother tongue or regional language be used as the primary medium of teaching throughout the secondary school stage, with the caveat that special accommodations be made for linguistic minorities.

Additionally, the Kothari Commission (1964–1966) said that at the college and university levels, mother tongue should be the medium of instruction.

In respect to this issue, Article 350A provides Facilities for instruction in mother-tongue at the primary stage. It states that

It shall be the endeavour of every State and of every local authority within the State to provide adequate facilities for instruction in the mother-tongue at the primary stage of education to children belonging to linguistic minority groups, and the President may issue such directions to any State as he considers necessary or proper for securing the provision of such facilities

Promotion of Hindi

The Indian Constitution calls for Hindi to be developed and promoted as the country's official language. Article 351 of the Indian constitution has a Directive for the development of the Hindi language.

Part of it states that it shall be the duty of the Union to promote the spread of the Hindi language, to develop it so that it may serve as a medium of expression for all the elements of the composite culture of India.

Additionally, the constitution stipulates the development and promotion of national languages, including Hindi.

According to article 351, it is the central government's specific responsibility to nurture Hindi language, in order for it to serve as a medium of expression for all the parts of India's composite culture. The Central Ministry of Home Affairs has a directorate of Hindi for this purpose.

Education in union territories

Article 239 of the constitution states," Save as otherwise provided by Parliament by how, every Union Territory shall be administered by the President acting to such extent as he thinks fit, through an administrator to be appointed by him with such designation as he may specify."

This means that each union territory has its own education department, and education in union territories has been the responsibility of the union or centre government.

Fundamental duty to provide the opportunity for education

Article 51A Clause 'K' – It shall be the duty of every citizen of India who is parent or guardian to provide opportunities for education to his child or as the case may be, wards between the age of six and fourteen years.

The Right to Education Act, 2009 makes it obligatory for state governments to ensure that all children have access to quality education.

Under Article 21 A every child between 6–14 years of age has the right to free and compulsory education in India. 'Compulsory education' makes the local authorities responsible for ensuring admission and completion of elementary education.

Article 28 gives students the freedom of attendance at any religious worship or participation in any religious instruction that may be imparted

The Right of Children to Free and Compulsory Education Act or Right to Education Act (RTE) is an Act Parliament of India enacted on 4 August 2009, which describes the modalities of the importance of free compulsory education children between the age of 6 to 14 years in India under Article 21A of the Indian Constitution India became one of 135 countries to make education a fundamental right of every child when the act came into force on 1 April 2010.

It requires all private schools(except the minority institutions) to reserve 25% of seats for the poor and other categories of children (to be reimbursed by the state as part of the public-private partnership plan).

A number of other provisions regarding improvement of school infrastructure, teacher-student ratio and faculty are made in the Act.

The Right to Education of persons with disabilities until 18 years of age is laid down under separate legislation-the Persons with Disabilities Act.

Constitutional Provisions for Education in India in Breif

The Indian constitution provides specifies provisions for education in the following major areas of education:

Provisions

1.Right of free and compulsory education Article 45

2.Right to education Article 21A

3.Education for women Article15(1) (3)

4.Promotion of education and economic interests of SC, ST and other weaker sections Article 46

5.Religious education Article 25, 28(1)(2)(3)

6.Education of minorities, protection of interests of minorities Article 29

7.Right of minorities to establish and administer educational institutions Article 30

8.Instruction in mother-tongue at the primary stage Article 350-A

9.Promotion of Hindi Article 351

10.Education in union territories Article 239

11.Fundamental duty to provide the opportunity for education Article 51(A)

CHAPTER TEN

Child Rights and Human Rights

All human beings are born free and equal in dignity and rights."
Article 1, Universal Declaration of Human Rights

In the history of human rights, the rights of children are the most ratified. The United Nations Convention on the Rights of the Child (UNCRC) defines Child Rights as the minimum entitlements and freedoms that should be afforded to every citizen below the age of 18 regardless of race, national origin, colour, gender, language, religion, opinions, origin, wealth, birth status, disability, or other characteristics.

These rights encompass freedom of children and their civil rights, family environment, necessary healthcare and welfare, education, leisure and cultural activities and special protection measures. The UNCRC outlines the fundamental human rights that should be afforded to children in four broad classifications that suitably cover all civil, political, social, economic and cultural rights of every child:

Right to Survival:
• Right to be born
• Right to minimum standards of food, shelter and clothing
• Right to live with dignity
• Right to health care, to safe drinking water, nutritious food, a clean and safe environment, and information to help them stay healthy

Right to Protection:
• Right to be protected from all sorts of violence
• Right to be protected from neglect
• Right to be protected from physical and sexual abuse
• Right to be protected from dangerous drugs

Right to Participation:
• Right to freedom of opinion
• Right to freedom of expression
• Right to freedom of association
• Right to information
• Right to participate in any decision making that involves him/her directly or indirectly

Right to Development:
• Right to education
• Right to learn
• Right to relax and play
• Right to all forms of development – emotional, mental and physical

Impact of the Convention of the Child Rights

A milestone in the international human rights legislation, the 'Convention on the Rights of the Child' has been instrumental in putting all the issues pertaining to children issues on the global as well as national agenda. In addition to this, it has extensively mobilized actions for the realization of the rights and development of children worldwide.

It was not an overnight initiative that resulted in the adoption of the Child Rights. It took several years of movements and activism on shaping favourable, positive and constructive attitudes toward children, and also inciting actions to improve their well-being. The enormous efforts involved toward the implementation of the Convention, the significant amount of resources committed to this cause, and the overall effectiveness of the systems put in place for the execution process have a bearing on the success of child well-being outcomes.

Over the last 20 or so years, implementation of the Convention and its effect on child well-being varied from country to country and from one region of the world to the other. Based on analysis, there has been outstanding progress at a global level in addressing the issues related to children. These include progress in access to services, reaching their fullest potential through education, enactment of laws that upholds the principle of the best interests of child, and child survival.

Though a noteworthy progress has been achieved, yet in developing countries, particularly India, there is still a long way to go in realising the rights of children. Though all the relevant rules and policies are in place, there is a lack in enforcement initiatives. As barriers, there are several factors that forbid effective implementation of the laws. Due to relatively low success in achieving concrete child development outcomes in India, the condition of underprivileged kids and underprivileged youth is harsh and needs urgent attention. There is a need to intensify efforts for children welfare at all levels to implement the rules and provisions of the Convention and contribute to create a world suitable for children.

Child Rights and the world

People from across the world striving for social justice have often directed their efforts toward the most vulnerable in society—the children. From Princess Diana's charitable work on behalf of children to the efforts of activists like Grace Abbott and the youngest Nobel laureate in history—Ms. Malala Yousafzai, these famous children's right activists have put commendable efforts in helping improve the lives of the youngest citizens.

2014 Nobel Peace Prize awardees—Ms. Malala Yousafzai and Mr. Kailash Satyarthi have reminded us all of the need to keep on advancing in providing opportunities that has an important effect on all children. The opportunities are meant to be meaningful enough to allow them to learn and gain the mindsets and skills that would empower them to be free, develop themselves, their communities and the world.

Mr. Kailash Satyarthi's struggle to liberate children from child labour had cost him many life threats, including bullet wounds by those who exploit young boys and girls for economic gain. Wearing flak jackets, and armed with strong determination, he and his team raided many illegal factories and mines to rescue the children who are sold into servitude. It has been 30 years now since he started his movement. A movement that has one clear purpose—no child shall be a slave.

On the other hand, when one thinks of Ms. Malala Yousafzai, the first thing that pops in one's mind is education. The second is—education for girls. In 2009, when she was just 11, she wrote to BBC about the norm of banning female education under the Taliban regime in the Swat Valley (her hometown). Her article gained tremendous momentum worldwide. She started her fight for the education of girls at that small age and began to speak publicly and to the press, which caused her and her family receive constant death threats.

"I strongly feel that this is a big honour to hundreds of millions of the children who have been deprived of their childhood and freedom and education." – Mr. Kailash Satyarthi.

"I speak not for myself but for those without voice... those who have fought for their rights... their right to live in peace, their right to be treated with dignity, their right to equality of opportunity, their right to be educated." – Ms. Malala Yousafzai.

The Right to Education

The father of modern education—John Amos Comenius proposed – "all persons should be educated, so we could have peace in the world". Visionaries of the world understood that peace meant guaranteeing every person certain rights that are conditional for humanity—education being one of the most important.

The addition of the Right to Education (RTE) in the Universal Declaration of Human Rights in 1948 was the beginning of a remarkable expansion of educational opportunities around the world. The parliament of India enacted the Right of Children to Free and Compulsory Education Act or Right to Education Act (RTE) on August 2009. The same got enforced on April 1st 2010.

As per the act, education is a fundamental right of every child who is between 6 and 14 years old. The act also states that until the completion of elementary education, no child shall be held back, expelled or required to pass a board examination. There is also a provision for special training of school drop-outs to bring them up to par with students of the same age.

As a charity for child rights, Smile Foundation has been providing education to marginalized children in poor rural and urban communities in 25 states of the country. Its flagship programme - Mission Education exemplifies the global struggle for universal education. The programme has succeeded in bringing more than 200,000 children to school since its start in the year 2002.

Underprivileged kids lag at all stages of education. When earning a livelihood and taking care of the members of the family becomes a primary matter of concern in one's life, education stands a little or, very often, no chance of pursuance. For the millions of underprivileged people in India, education is a high-priced luxury, and this negative outlook continues on with every new generation. Poverty damages childhood with significant effects on a child's physical and mental health, as well as educational achievement. It limits the expectations of the child's ability to perform well in school, constantly reminding him/her of the miniscule chance he/she has to overcome adversity and poverty.

With its development interventions that are focused on social welfare of children, Smile Foundation has raised those expectations among the hardest-to-reach children. Recent mark-sheets of the students in all ME centres has shown Smile Foundation primary school students outperforming their peers, with a very high passing rate. Last year, 51% of the total beneficiaries in Mission Education centres across India were girls. Also, 87% of the total eligible students are successfully mainstreamed in private and government schools.

Summary of UNCRC

Article 1

Everyone under 18 years of age has all the rights in this Convention.

Article 2

The Convention applies to everyone whatever their race, religion, abilities, whatever they think or say, whatever type of family they come from.

Article 3

All organisations concerned with children should work towards what is best for each child.

Article 4

Governments should make these rights available to children.

Article 5

Governments should respect the rights and responsibilities of families to direct and guide their children so that, as they grow, they learn to use their rights properly.

Article 6

All children have the right to life. Governments should ensure that children survive and develop healthily.

Article 7

All children have the right to a legally registered name, and nationality. They have the right to know and, as far as possible, to be cared for, by their parents.

Article 8

Governments should respect children's right to a name, a nationality and family ties.

Article 9

Children should not be separated from their parents unless it is for their own good (for example if a parent is mistreating or neglecting a child.) Children whose parents have separated have the right to stay in contact with both parents, unless this might harm the child.

Article 10

Families who live in different countries should be allowed to move between those countries so that parents and children can stay in contact, or get back together as a family.

Article 11

Governments should take steps to stop children being taken out of their own country illegally.

Article 12

Children have the right to say what they think should happen, when adults are making decisions that affect them, and to have their opinions taken into account.

Article 13

Children have the right to get and to share information, as long as the information is not damaging to them or to others.

Article 14

Children have the right to think and believe what they want, and to practise their religion, as long as they are not stopping other people from enjoying their rights. Parents should guide their children on these matters.

Article 15

Children have the right to meet together and to join groups and organisations, as long as this does not stop other people from enjoying their rights.

Article 16

Children have a right to privacy. The law should protect them from attacks against their way of life, their good name, their families and their homes.

Article 17

Children have the right to reliable information from the mass media. Television, radio, and newspapers should provide information that children can understand, and should not promote materials that could harm children.

Article 18

Both parents share responsibility for bringing up their children, and should always consider what is best for each child. Governments should help parents by providing services to support them, especially if both parents work outside the home.

Article 19

Governments should ensure that children are properly cared for, and protect them from violence, abuse and neglect by their parents, or anyone else who looks after them.

Article 20

Children who cannot be looked after by their own family must be looked after properly, by people who respect their religion, culture and language.

Article 21

When children are adopted the first concern must be what is best for them. The same rules should apply whether the children are adopted in the country where they were born, or if they are taken to live in another country.

Article 22

Children who come into a country as refugees should have the same rights as children born in that country.

Article 23

Children who have any kind of disability should have special care and support, so that they can lead full and independent lives.

Article 24

Children have the right to good quality health care, to clean water, nutritious food, and a clean environment, so that they will stay healthy. Rich countries should help poorer countries achieve this.

Article 25

Children who are looked after by their local authority, rather than by their parents, should have someone review the situation regularly.

Article 26

The Government should provide extra money for the children of families in need.

Article 27

Children have a right to a standard of living that is good enough to meet their physical and mental needs. The Government should help families who cannot afford to provide this.

Article 28

Children have a right to an education. Discipline in schools should respect children's human dignity. Primary education should be free. Wealthy countries should help poorer countries achieve this.

Article 29

Education should develop each child's personality and talents to the full. It should encourage children to respect their parents, and their own and other cultures.

Article 30

Children have a right to learn and use the language and customs of their families, whether these are shared by the majority of people in the country or not.

Article 31

All children have a right to relax and play, and to join in a wide range of activities.

Article 32

The Government should protect children from work that is dangerous, or that might harm their health or their education.

Article 33

The Government should provide ways of protecting children from dangerous drugs.

Article 34

The Government should protect children from sexual abuse.

Article 35

The Government should make sure that children are not abducted or sold.

Article 36

Children should be protected from any activities that could harm their development.

Article 37

Children who break the law should not be treated cruelly. They should not be put in prison with adults and should be able to keep in contact with their families.

Article 38

Governments should not allow children under 15 to join the army. Children in war zones should receive special protection.

Article 39

Children who have been neglected or abused should receive special help to restore their self-respect.

Article 40

Children who are accused of breaking the law should receive legal help. Prison sentences for children should only be used for the most serious offences.

Article 41

If the laws of a particular country protect children better than the articles of the Convention, then those laws should stay.

Article 42

The Government should make the Convention known to all parents and children

Universal Declaration of Human Rights

The Universal Declaration of Human Rights (UDHR) is a milestone document in the history of human rights. Drafted by representatives with different legal and cultural backgrounds from all regions of the world, the Declaration was proclaimed by the United Nations General Assembly in Paris on 10 December 1948 (General Assembly resolution 217 A) as a common standard of achievements for all peoples and all nations. It sets out, for the first time, fundamental human rights to be universally protected and it has been translated into over 500 languages. The UDHR is widely recognized as having inspired, and paved the way for, the adoption of more than seventy human rights treaties, applied today on a permanent basis at global and regional levels (all containing references to it in their preambles).

Preamble

Whereas recognition of the inherent dignity and of the equal and inalienable rights of all members of the human family is the foundation of freedom, justice and peace in the world,

Whereas disregard and contempt for human rights have resulted in barbarous acts which have outraged the conscience of mankind, and the advent of a world in which human beings shall enjoy freedom of speech and belief and freedom from fear and want has been proclaimed as the highest aspiration of the common people,

Whereas it is essential, if man is not to be compelled to have recourse, as a last resort, to rebellion against tyranny and oppression, that human rights should be protected by the rule of law,

Whereas it is essential to promote the development of friendly relations between nations,

Whereas the peoples of the United Nations have in the Charter reaffirmed their faith in fundamental human rights, in the dignity and worth of the human person and in the equal rights of men and women and have determined to promote social progress and better standards of life in larger freedom,

Whereas Member States have pledged themselves to achieve, in co-operation with the United Nations, the promotion of universal respect for and observance of human rights and fundamental freedoms,

Whereas a common understanding of these rights and freedoms is of the greatest importance for the full realization of this pledge,

Now, therefore,

The General Assembly,

Proclaims this Universal Declaration of Human Rights as a common standard of achievement for all peoples and all nations, to the end that every individual and every organ of society, keeping this Declaration constantly in mind, shall strive by teaching and education to promote respect for these rights and freedoms and by progressive measures, national and international, to secure their universal and effective recognition and observance, both among the peoples of Member States themselves and among the peoples of territories under their jurisdiction.

Article 1

All human beings are born free and equal in dignity and rights. They are endowed with reason and conscience and should act towards one another in a spirit of brotherhood.

Article 2

Everyone is entitled to all the rights and freedoms set forth in this Declaration, without distinction of any kind, such as race, colour, sex, language, religion, political or other opinion, national or social origin, property, birth or other status. Furthermore, no distinction shall be made on the basis of the political, jurisdictional or international status of the country or territory to which a person belongs, whether it be independent, trust, non-self-governing or under any other limitation of sovereignty.

Article 3

Everyone has the right to life, liberty and security of person.

Article 4

No one shall be held in slavery or servitude; slavery and the slave trade shall be prohibited in all their forms.

Article 5

No one shall be subjected to torture or to cruel, inhuman or degrading treatment or punishment.

Article 6

Everyone has the right to recognition everywhere as a person before the law.

Article 7

All are equal before the law and are entitled without any discrimination to equal protection of the law. All are entitled to equal protection against any discrimination in violation of this Declaration and against any incitement to such discrimination.

Article 8

Everyone has the right to an effective remedy by the competent national tribunals for acts violating the fundamental rights granted him by the constitution or by law.

Article 9

No one shall be subjected to arbitrary arrest, detention or exile.

Article 10

Everyone is entitled in full equality to a fair and public hearing by an independent and impartial tribunal, in the determination of his rights and obligations and of any criminal charge against him.

Article 11

Everyone charged with a penal offence has the right to be presumed innocent until proved guilty according to law in a public trial at which he has had all the guarantees necessary for his defence.

No one shall be held guilty of any penal offence on account of any act or omission which did not constitute a penal offence, under national or international law, at the time when it was committed. Nor shall a heavier penalty be imposed than the one that was applicable at the time the penal offence was committed.

Article 12

No one shall be subjected to arbitrary interference with his privacy, family, home or correspondence, nor to attacks upon his honour and reputation. Everyone has the right to the protection of the law against such interference or attacks.

Article 13

Everyone has the right to freedom of movement and residence within the borders of each state.

Everyone has the right to leave any country, including his own, and to return to his country.

Article 14

Everyone has the right to seek and to enjoy in other countries asylum from persecution.

This right may not be invoked in the case of prosecutions genuinely arising from non-political crimes or from acts contrary to the purposes and principles of the United Nations.

Article 15

Everyone has the right to a nationality.

No one shall be arbitrarily deprived of his nationality nor denied the right to change his nationality.

Article 16

Men and women of full age, without any limitation due to race, nationality or religion, have the right to marry and to found a family. They are entitled to equal rights as to marriage, during marriage and at its dissolution.

Marriage shall be entered into only with the free and full consent of the intending spouses.

The family is the natural and fundamental group unit of society and is entitled to protection by society and the State.

Article 17

Everyone has the right to own property alone as well as in association with others.

No one shall be arbitrarily deprived of his property.

Article 18

Everyone has the right to freedom of thought, conscience and religion; this right includes freedom to change his religion or belief, and freedom, either alone or in community with others and in public or private, to manifest his religion or belief in teaching, practice, worship and observance.

Article 19

Everyone has the right to freedom of opinion and expression; this right includes freedom to hold opinions without interference and to seek, receive and impart information and ideas through any media and regardless of frontiers.

Article 20

Everyone has the right to freedom of peaceful assembly and association.

No one may be compelled to belong to an association.

Article 21

Everyone has the right to take part in the government of his country, directly or through freely chosen representatives.

Everyone has the right of equal access to public service in his country.

The will of the people shall be the basis of the authority of government; this will shall be expressed in periodic and genuine elections which shall be by universal and equal suffrage and shall be held by secret vote or by equivalent free voting procedures.

Article 22

Everyone, as a member of society, has the right to social security and is entitled to realization, through national effort and international co-operation and in accordance with the organization and resources of each State, of the economic, social and cultural rights indispensable for his dignity and the free development of his personality.

Article 23

Everyone has the right to work, to free choice of employment, to just and favourable conditions of work and to protection against unemployment.

Everyone, without any discrimination, has the right to equal pay for equal work.

Everyone who works has the right to just and favourable remuneration ensuring for himself and his family an existence worthy of human dignity, and supplemented, if necessary, by other means of social protection.

Everyone has the right to form and to join trade unions for the protection of his interests.

Article 24

Everyone has the right to rest and leisure, including reasonable limitation of working hours and periodic holidays with pay.

Article 25

Everyone has the right to a standard of living adequate for the health and well-being of himself and of his family, including food, clothing, housing and medical care and necessary social services, and the right to security in the event of unemployment, sickness, disability, widowhood, old age or other lack of livelihood in circumstances beyond his control.

Motherhood and childhood are entitled to special care and assistance. All children, whether born in or out of wedlock, shall enjoy the same social protection.

Article 26

Everyone has the right to education. Education shall be free, at least in the elementary and fundamental stages. Elementary education shall be compulsory. Technical and professional education shall be made generally available and higher education shall be equally accessible to all on the basis of merit.

Education shall be directed to the full development of the human personality and to the strengthening of respect for human rights and fundamental freedoms. It shall promote understanding, tolerance and friendship among all nations, racial or religious groups, and shall further the activities of the United Nations for the maintenance of peace.

Parents have a prior right to choose the kind of education that shall be given to their children.

Article 27

Everyone has the right freely to participate in the cultural life of the community, to enjoy the arts and to share in scientific advancement and its benefits.

Everyone has the right to the protection of the moral and material interests resulting from any scientific, literary or artistic production of which he is the author.

Article 28

Everyone is entitled to a social and international order in which the rights and freedoms set forth in this Declaration can be fully realized.

Article 29

Everyone has duties to the community in which alone the free and full development of his personality is possible.

In the exercise of his rights and freedoms, everyone shall be subject only to such limitations as are determined by law solely for the purpose of securing due recognition and respect for the rights and freedoms of others and of meeting the just requirements of morality, public order and the general welfare in a democratic society.

These rights and freedoms may in no case be exercised contrary to the purposes and principles of the United Nations.

Article 30

Nothing in this Declaration may be interpreted as implying for any State, group or person any right to engage in any activity or to perform any act aimed at the destruction of any of the rights and freedoms set forth herein.

References

Maheswari, V. K. (2012). Education of the deprived/ marginalized groups. Retrieved from http://www.vkmaheshwari.com/WP/?p=569.

Padhi, S.R. (2016). Overcoming Exclusion and Marginalization in Education through Inclusive Approaches: Challenges and Vision of Arunachal Pradesh in India. International Journal of Social Science and Humanity, Vol. 6 (4)

Ramesh (2013). Levels of education of the marginalized people in India. International Journal of Social Science & Interdisciplinary Research. Vol. 2 (3)

Saksena D.(2014). The Problems of Marginalized Groups in India. Retrieved from https://www.lawctopus.com/academike/problems-marginalized-groups-india/

Census of India, 2011, published on NITI Aayog (http://niti.gov.in)

Government of India, (2012), "Employment and Unemployment Situation among Social Groups in India", NSS 66th Round, National Sample Survey Organisation, New Delhi https://www.hrw.org/report/2014/04/22/.../denying-education-indias-marginalized

https://timesofindia.indiatimes.com/readersblog/word-toon-nia/education-as-the-perfect-instrument-for-social-change-38659/

https://ir.nbu.ac.in/bitstream/123456789/4006/1/IJLJ%20%20Vol.%2011%20No.%201%20%28Part%20III%29%20Article%20No%206.pdf

http://ijrar.com/upload_issuc/ijrar_issue_1520.pdf